Faith and Contemplation

BY THE SAME AUTHOR

Brothers of Men
The Need for Contemplation
Christian Vocation

Faith and Contemplation

RENÉ VOILLAUME

DIMENSION BOOKS
Denville, New Jersey

Published by:

DIMENSION BOOKS, INC.
Denville, New Jersey 07834

First published as
Ou Est Votre Foi?
by Editions du Cerf, Paris
This translation first published 1974 and
© *Darton, Longman and Todd Ltd*

ISBN 0 232 51256 6

Contents

Contents

Preface

The talks which make up this book were given at a retreat
for lay people, mostly belonging to the "Secular Fraternity"
a group within the spiritual family of Charles de Foucauld.

It is at the request of the people on that retreat that
these talks are now being published. Despite being trans-
cribed and edited, the text retains the faults inherent in
any oral communication which is subsequently turned over
to be printed. On the other hand the style does perhaps
convey something of the directness of approach which I
tried to maintain at the retreat.

The reader will remember that these are addresses given
during the course of a retreat and he should not expect to
find carefully expounded teaching on the subjects touched
upon. I was concerned rather to set the problems in
relation to the lives of Christians, living as a brotherhood
in the world today.

A printed text cannot of course convey the atmosphere
of a retreat nor the real spirit of the ensuing discussion and
the questioning which helped to clarify the points I was
trying to make.

In spite of this, I hope that these thoughts will be of
some use to those Christians who want to rethink the
meaning and nature of faith, as members of the Church, in
their vocations as sons of God and in relation to the needs
of men in our world today.

Saint-Julien
January 1971

I

Faith, a Response

Faith is the mark of the Christian. Faith in Jesus Christ, Son of God and Son of Man, Jesus Christ the Saviour, crucified and risen, living in his Church in order to set up the Kingdom of God in charity and love among men. In sum it is adherence to all that the Creed affirms. But I can hear already a number of questions! Someone will say, "Is it really faith that marks the Christian? Is it not rather the perfecting of love?" To which I should answer, "No, it is faith!"

Certainly love, perfect love, is the supreme demand to the Christian. If you do not love, you are not acting in conformity with your calling as a Christian. Yet, if you have faith, even without the perfection of charity, you are all the same a Christian. Further, life can be lived by the grace of Christ, and, even in a Christian perspective, by men who do not have an explicit faith in Christ, who perhaps do not even know him. There are non-Christians who have more charity than Christians. But the Christian, even if he be a bad one, so long as he has faith in Christ, is a Christian.

When you take your small child to be baptized, you are asked the question, "What do you ask of Christ?", and you reply, "Faith."

What then is faith?

There are those who say they have faith, while others

say they do not. Some say they have lost faith, as one loses any other thing! And they speak as if there was nothing in this loss!

Others, on the contrary, have "found" faith in God, as one finds a treasure, and this finding seems then to be something exceptionally important for the life of a man. It is a moment which stands out in life, the first moment of being enlightened by faith.

They also speak of "dead faith" and "living faith", and sometimes that we have to "live by faith".

All these ways of speaking show that we are dealing with a deeply mysterious reality in the heart of man. And this faith seems to us all the more inexplicable in that it is set within us, not only to justify itself, but to make itself clear, to say what it is.

Now let us look at faith, not from the angle of him who possesses it but in itself. What is the reality to which faith leads us? We know that, if we want to know something about the purpose of existence, about the way we ought to live, we can only, if we are Christians, do this in the context of faith. We cannot leave faith aside, for without it we cannot be Christians.

I should like to begin with the Bible. For the Bible speaks to us of faith : we might even define the Bible as a summary of the history of faith among men. I shall speak first of the Old Testament faith, then in the next chapter of faith in Jesus Christ. I have not yet defined faith : I would rather leave such a definition till after I have examined the biblical evidence.

Some say that man is a religious being. They hold that religious feeling is something which is part of human nature, in all cultures and all civilizations. The fact that he is religious does not mean that a man has faith, at any rate in the full sense in which we understand it here. However I would say that the fact of being religious is for man a sort of basis for faith, and leads on towards faith. This is why, when we begin the story of the faith of mankind, we have to set ourselves in the context of the period. For then all men were in some sense religious; they had a religion, whatever that religion was.

Faith begins when God manifests himself in human history so as to accomplish therein his plan of salvation. So God does not reveal himself to an unintelligent universe, he reveals himself to men, and faith began just at this moment of the summons to man by God. Faith is the response to that call. We might even say that it is the universal response of man. By saying this I mean that when God begins to carry out his plan of salvation in human history, his call concerns all men and all humanity as such, even when this call is addressed first to certain individuals.

Let us look at the facts as the Bible tells them to us. The first event is the call made to Abraham. He, like the men of his time, believed in divine beings. Idolatry reigned everywhere, and each people had its national gods.

God revealed himself to Abraham, and sought from him not complicated things (or such as he could not understand), but deeds in the context of his day to day life. Abraham was a nomad : God demanded from him that he go on his way. Abraham responded with an act of obedience; he did simply what God asked him. This was the first mark of his faith in God, a faith which was first of all obedience.

But God went on to call for something further : he asked Abraham to believe in the promises which he would make to him. God promised him a lineage, and enabled him to see that this would become a people. It was a mysterious plan which was revealed to Abraham, and which seemed to extend to future generations. Nothing could touch the heart of a man of the time of Abraham like his name being carried on in future generations : "I will make you a great nation, . . . I will multiply your descendants as the stars of heaven and as the sand which is on the seashore" (Gen. 12. 2; 22. 16–17). For this he must have a son; but Sara was advanced in years and she could no longer have a child. But God's promise was followed by the declaration of the coming birth of a son. You know the reaction of Sara : "Sara laughed to herself saying, After I have grown old and my husband is old, shall I have this pleasure?" And the following year the promise came true; Sara bore a son.

But God is to go still further. It seems that the unique thing that God demanded from Abraham was not perfection according to a moral code but the offering of his whole being, of his entire life in unconditional faithfulness to Yahweh who had revealed himself to him. He had to be utterly obedient to the whole design of God. It is then that we witness that mysterious event, the meaning of which is dramatic and crucial : the sacrifice of the child of promise, at the very hands of the father who was still to believe in the promise! God made the gift, but God demanded the sacrifice of that same gift, without Abraham asking himself how the promise was then to come true. It seemed that his faith in the Word of God had more value than the object of the promise.

This event, even in its historic context, had very deep meaning. This act of blind faith in his promise was the means of redemption. "Abraham believed God, and it was counted to him for righteousness", Saint Paul tells us (Rom. 4. 9.). We are in a quite different sphere. You see how one question raises another. How is man justified in the eyes of God? We would have judged Abraham very harshly for his moral attitudes yet God introduced him to two great realities – his faithfulness and his omnipotence.

Yes, God is faithful! Whatever happens we have to believe despite all appearances and all hope. It is precisely this attitude of faith that God elicited in Abraham. This thought of God's faithfulness is closely bound up with that of his omnipotence. God can do all.

Abraham is rightly called the Father of Believers. The three great religions, Judaism, Islam and Christianity, all look to Abraham, whose faith marks a stage in the relations between man and God; it inaugurated the realization of God's plan of salvation.

Let us now look at the faith of Israel.

It was demanded by the Covenant, which was confirmed through an historical event, of great importance for Israel – the deliverance from Egypt. If we want to understand the history of Israel and its place in the design of God, we have to read the Old Testament passages concerning Moses, at the time of the Exodus and the period in the desert. These events are extremely important, not only for knowing Israel, its soul, its reactions, its religious history and what the Covenant meant for it, but also for understanding Jesus Christ.

In the story of Moses, as in that of Abraham, it was God who took the initiative. A second phase of the realization of God's plan was to begin. Once again, God showed himself and expected in response a total faith.

You remember how, at the time of his revelation to Moses, who was then a shepherd and guarded the flocks of Jethro his father-in-law, God presented himself to him as the God of Abraham. The call of God to Moses was directly related to that of Abraham. It was not just any god who was speaking to him; "I am the God of your father, the God of Abraham, the God of Isaac and the God of Jacob" (Exod. 3. 6). Much time had passed since the call to Abraham. It seemed as if the thread was broken.

However Moses appeared to be a timid man : he was afraid of God's call, for he did not feel that he had the capacity to take his people in hand. (Exod. 4. 10). He appealed to God who allowed him to be accompanied by his brother Aaron; he it was who spoke in Moses's name and in his stead.

At every stage God used Moses to free Israel from slavery in Egypt. It was a difficult process which looked at times to be impossible, but throughout God called for trust and perseverance, so that this freeing of the chosen people should be seen to be the exclusive work of the Power of

God, making use of the weakness of human beings. This same lesson of faith, of trust in God and of abandonment to his omnipotence, is continually recalled to Israel by the events of its history.

Moses then became the mediator with Israel. It was by his intervention that the pact of the Covenant was renewed, at the time of the revelation of the glory of God on Sinai.

Moses was an important figure, glorified by the privilege of having encountered God face to face, from having seen the Invisible.

From this time onwards, the Covenant involved more precise demands. Henceforth the whole people would have to obey the word of God after the manner set forth in the commandments given on Sinai. This was the real Code of Covenant. Israel was to obey; it had to follow the divine injunctions and it had to believe in Yahweh, the unique God, in face of the constant temptations to idolatry rising from its past, and from the religious beliefs of surrounding peoples. It would have to be faithful, and that would not be easy! For, to make this faithfulness strong, God tested it many times. The pattern was always the same : the exodus, the long time in the desert, marked by rebellions of the people, thirsty, hungry, wanting to go back, feeling the desire to get settled.

Yet, it is precisely through the demands of nomadic life for detachment, for hardship and the uncertainty of to-morrow that God forged the soul of his people. This was why this event was so important for the faith of Israel in its God. The psalms and the religious rituals continually reminded Israel of the coming forth from Egypt. It was a miracle which demonstrated the power of God over his people. It was a sure sign of the Covenant. It testified to the great acts of God, which the children of Israel must never forget; and lastly it was a proof of the love which God had for his people.

This faith would constantly be exposed to temptations, against which the prophets continually warn. Idolatry was one such temptation. To understand the gravity and the strength of this temptation, we have to turn and look at the religious mentality of men at this period : each people had its special and protecting divinities. Israel was surrounded by these idolatrous peoples, whose urban civilization was often further advanced than their own. They had either to conquer these peoples or else submit to their influence.

Another temptation against which the prophets had to struggle was that of religious formalism. They never ceased to recall the demands of the divine law, especially the demands of love and justice to one's neighbour.

Finally, other temptations arose from the conviction that Israel was specially elected. It knew itself to be the promised people. Thus it was always concerned to overpower surrounding peoples who threatened its independence. This was the temptation to achieve salvation by human force. But God wanted Israel to prove its faith and trust in divine aid, even when it was in a state of weakness. It must resist the temptation to enter into military alliances with people stronger than itself at times when it was threatened with invasion. The whole history of Israel was underwritten by these divine demands.

What then is the content of this faith of Israel? The content is simple : Israel believes in a unique God, creator of the world yet distinct from the world. Since the revelation made to Moses, and contained in the five books of the Pentateuch, Israel cannot doubt this.

Its God is also the Lord of history and especially of its own history. Up till the time of the Kings the people were especially clear that they had no head but God himself. Whenever Israel relied on its own power to determine its own history, God reacted by interventions, which were often catastrophic for her.

Finally, God is for Israel the Faithful One. They called him the Rock, the one on whom they could and should lean in complete trust. By the trials which this trust went through, the people developed a purified feeling of hope and an expectation of a Saviour. The exile of Israel, the wreck of the kingdom and the ruin of the Temple were decisive in this sense.

But what exactly was the hope of Israel? What was this new Israel and the kingdom to come of which the prophets told? After each test, the object of their hope came into sharper relief. There would be the return from Babylonian captivity and the rebuilding of the Temple. But after that? Through the great prophets there came the mysterious word of an Israel to come, an Israel which expanded to some kind of universality, a kingdom glorious and lasting. Above all there was the image of the Messiah which was sketched out : a contradictory image, deformed by nationalistic aspirations, the image of the King of Glory, and at the same time, an image of sorrow, not so clearly defined in the imagination of most of the believers in Israel – the image of the Suffering Servant of Yahweh.

True, the faith of Israel was limited, imperfect, obscure. It was imperfect, because it was interpreted in a temporal sense, at least by the majority. It was imperfect because it was clouded with legalism, the inevitable result of the extremely scrupulous observance of the Law. It was imperfect because it was at every moment, subject to the temptations of pride, to a complaisance in its own perfection – pharisaism. Such was· the context into which Jesus Christ came! But what then is faith? What stage has been reached?

In the Old Testament faith comprised a notion of solidarity and at the same time of security and confidence. This stands out clearly in all we have said about the calling of Abraham and of Israel.

But this feeling of confidence, of yielding to the plan of God, was accompanied by a more complete knowledge of God. For God in manifesting himself let himself be known as he was. Faith is a feeling of trust which is addressed to a person who is faithful, to a personal God towards whom one pledges all one's being, all one's existence. But faith also produces and demands a pledge of the whole man. This is why faith is not just simple and definable. This pledge cannot be something blind, because faith has to be the act of free mankind – without this it would have no value for God – and this cannot come to pass without some element of knowledge. Through his acts, words and signs God introduces man to invisible realities which man cannot know by himself. It is the whole countenance of God which the Bible story reveals. And this countenance has a name, the acts of which show forth "the ways of God".

II

Our Faith in Jesus Christ

This faith is clarified, purified, deepened, and its object explained by faith in Jesus Christ. Since the dawn, if I may so put it, of the New Testament, the event which immediately preceded the birth of Christ, the message to Zachariah and the birth of John the Baptist, carries already a kind of purification of faith. For Zachariah, even as Mary, is called upon to believe. It is a remarkable thing, that the whole New Testament story rests on this double call to faith. Zachariah is even punished for not having believed. We always have to remember the almighty fruitfulness of the Word of God. John the Baptist is to be born against all hope.

On the contrary with the announcement of the Messiah made to Mary, we enter another world. Mary's faith has a unique quality. We are already in Christ's world, it is already truly the world of the Word made flesh. We must meditate much on this mystery of the Annunciation to Mary : by mystery I understand an event whose hidden and deep meaning God shows us.

We have already said that faith is the response of man to the plan of God, and this may be most clearly seen in the dialogue between Mary and the angel who announces the Incarnation to her.

There is in it a clearness of intention and a very great purity of abandonment to God. Mary believed in what had been said to her as an indisputable truth : she knew that it was the Messiah that she bore within her. She believed.

And it is then, in the full sense of the word, the total giving
of her person – that God may do with her what he wills :
"I am at his entire disposition !" She will put only such
questions as seem to her indispensable to regulate her conduct. Was she to be a mother ? How should this be ? Beyond
this question, and with its mysterious and seemingly impossible aswer, Mary asks no more. "I am the Lord's servant;
be it unto me according to Thy word."

John the Baptist, rightly named the forerunner, is a man
of simple yet strong faith. Nothing is more touching than to
see with what simplicity, after announcing the Christ, he
fades out. He has the strength of soul to let his disciples
leave him to go and join those of Christ. In the faithfulness
of his mission as forerunner, nothing is more human than
the doubts which pass through his heart and his understanding, even when he was in prison for having preached
too vehemently.

And so he finds himself tested by doubt. Messiah ? But
why does he not manifest himself ? Nothing is happening
in the way he, John, would have expected it.

Even a man like John the Baptist is bewildered by the
physiognomy of Christ. You know how from prison he was
to send messengers to the Lord, to ask him, "Are you he
who is to come, or shall we look for another?" (Matt.
11. 3).

And you know Christ's answer : "The blind receive their
sight, and the lame walk, lepers are cleansed and the deaf
hear, and the dead are raised up, and the poor have the good
news preached to them. And blessed is he who takes no
offence in me." (Matt. 11. 5–6). Strange words for John
awaiting all the same for something more than miracles !
But these are signs. There will always be, in the movement
which is to lead faithful souls to Christ, a zone of darkness.
Yes, even in John the Baptist, faith did not shut out the
test of doubt. For when he had given the answer to John's
envoys, Jesus went on to express his admiration of the
Baptist.

So Jesus manifests himself. The people of Galilee, of Judaea, of Palestine are to have the privilege, the possibility of hearing and seeing Christ. They will hear and see him, but what will be their faith?

As I have already said regarding faith in the Old Testament, one has to place oneself in the context of the time to understand the questions that the Jews, Christ's contemporaries, naturally asked about him, and what difficulties they would have to overcome in order to believe in him.

For it is good for us to remind ourselves that the people's faith in God, in Yahweh, was profound, for it was a firm belief in the transcendence of the God of Sinai. All Israelites who drew near to Christ believed in God and believed with simplicity in the reality of prophecy. To see in Jesus a prophet offered them no difficulty, for he set forth his teaching by word and performed miracles to authenticate his teaching. But what did Jesus mean when he demanded that men should believe in him? What was the content of this faith of the first disciples?

We are told that when Jesus performed at Cana his first miracle, "His disciples believed him" (John 2. 11). That could be interpreted in many ways. It could mean that they thought that Jesus was invested with divine power, since he performed miracles. But these miracles meant something. There was then a discussion to know whether Jesus was really sent by God or not. Think of the story of the healing of the man born blind, and of the discussion which followed, between the poor man and his parents on the one hand, and the teachers of the law on the other (John 9. 1–41). Jesus had healed on the sabbath day! He ought not to have done so. The man is logical in his simplicity. "Never has it been said that anyone opened the eyes of one blind from birth." It would be very difficult to think that Jesus could have done it save by the power of God. And if God is with him, how could he lead us astray? Such is man's logic, a logic which leads to faith.

On their part the doctors of the law say, "This man is

not from God, since he does not keep the sabbath." As regards his parents, they dare not commit themselves through fear of getting into trouble with the religious authorities. "He is of age ! Ask him !"

This means that, from the beginning and throughout the life of Christ, to believe in Jesus Christ was to be in trouble. When the poor folk, the weak, the deaf, the blind or the lame begged Christ to heal them, Jesus first appealed to their faith (Luke 7. 50 : "All is possible to him that believes." Mark 9. 22 : "I believe. Help thou mine unbelief"). Further, it was said that Jesus did not perform miracles when he did not find round him sufficient faith. It was so at Nazareth, his own home. "He did not many miracles there, because of their lack of faith." (Matt. 13. 58).

It is a question of faith in the all-powerfulness of Christ.

At other times it was a question of accepting his teaching and putting it into practice, that is, believing in the truth of his words. But it is hard to affirm that it was a question in all cases of believing "who he was". There is the dialogue between Jesus and the centurion, a Roman (Matt. 8. 8–13) : he is not a Jew, but he begins to recognize in Christ a power of supernatural origin. This was the first step towards recognizing a divine mission, and then of adhering to the teaching of Christ.

That centurion's faith in the power of Christ is complete : it is a divine power, for it operates observably, without explanation. He is an officer, and he knows what authority means and what it means to be obeyed. The Lord has authority, there is no need for him to put himself out : "Only say the word, and my servant will be healed . . ." When Jesus heard him, he marvelled, and said "Truly I say to you, not even in Israel have I found such faith."

In the same way he was full of wonder at the poor Canaanite woman when she came humbly to beg a favour from him : "O woman, great is thy faith" (Matt. 15 21–28). Jesus showed joy at stirring up in simple souls this open faith in his all-powerfulness.

But the thrust of faith goes further – it leads on to the fundamental question : "Who is Jesus Christ?"

Such a question had to be put. Many other prophets had worked miracles. Elijah had even restored the dead to life, but this only made people pay attention to his prophetic teaching. They were men raised up by God to remind the people of their obligation to conform to the demands of the Covenant.

But who was Jesus Christ? Was he not a prophet?

A number of signs and events led some people to think that he might perhaps be the Messiah so that was the first question asked : could he be the Messiah?

If we look carefully at the story of the call of the first Apostles, we note that this question was asked very quickly, and by some of them at the first meeting.

"We have found the Messiah" (John 1. 40–45), says Andrew to his brother Simon. They said to one another, "That which was spoken in the Law of Moses, this we have found!" The coming of the Messiah meant for them the end of the servitude of Israel, the departure of the Romans, the freeing of the people, the inauguration of a glorious and peaceful kingdom of Israel; all that would be awakened in the heart of true Israelites. This was a cause of serious difficulties in their dealings with Jesus.

These first disciples moved little by little to penetrate the secret of the person of Christ. If he is the Messiah then he is the Son of God, following the Bible which makes it a messianic title. This title can be understood in several ways. Son of God means also the man chosen by God. Faith in the Messiah did not then necessarily imply faith in the divinity of Christ, which is another thing! This comes to be understood little by little.

Jesus is then a prophet, but he does not teach like other prophets. The people are astonished, moved by his teaching : "He teaches as one having authority" (Matt. 7. 29).

The first demonstration of the authority of Christ was in

the Temple, when Jesus, at the age of twelve, amazed the
teachers of the law by his questions and answers, for these,
if they really were those of a child of twelve, were enlightened by a wisdom of divine origin. Such wisdom can
be seen at all ages, as soon as a man has come to what we
call the age of reason. This showing of wisdom was one of
the ways in which his parents discovered more and more
about the personality of their son, for this even for Mary
and Joseph remained a mystery. From this day forward
they went on discovering in their son the manifestation of
a personality which they had probably not suspected at the
beginning. Jesus' replies to his parents show him to be
astonished : it seemed quite natural to him that his parents
should know, that they had penetrated his secret : "How
is it that you sought me? Did you not know that I must be
in my Father's house?" (Luke 2. 49). We can easily understand how his mother and Joseph had difficulty in realizing
what was going on in the mind of their child.

An authority and a knowledge at once discreet and
exceptional showed in the way Jesus spoke, and it is that
which drew the crowds after him. It was not only the
miracles which attracted the crowds; it was perhaps the
way in which he taught them. They were captivated. The
people were all the more astonished when they knew that
Jesus had spent his whole life at Nazareth working and that
he had not studied the law like the scribes. Whence then
comes all this learning? asked the people of Nazareth
(Matt. 13. 53–56).

And Jesus began to speak to them about the Kingdom
of God. This is something of great importance to his
audience; a temporal messianic kingdom was possible. We
might say that up to the Passion the Apostles believed that
Jesus was going to set up again the Kingdom of Israel in
its glory. They were Israelites of their time! Their faith
was complex, for they believed also all that Jesus said to
them, but it was not clear to them. They remained attached
to Jesus even when they did not understand : "Lord, to

whom shall we go?" (John 6. 67–71). There were bound
to be contradictions in what they thought about Jesus; but
this was compatible with a total faith in the mystery of the
Person of their Master. And when Jesus asks them : "Who
do men say that the Son of Man is?" they reply that they
think he is a prophet. Then comes the more direct question
to Peter : "But for you, who am I?" – "You are the Christ,
the Son of God" (Matt. 16. 13–17). And we know that
these words meant to Peter something very different from
the more or less symbolic title that was used about the
prophets. This we see well from Christ's answer, "Happy
are you, Simon Bar-Jona, for this revelation has come to
you not by flesh and blood, but by my Father who is in
heaven." There was no need of a revelation to understand
the words Son of God in the traditional biblical sense.
Peter then had an intuition partly open to him alone; did
he alone have at that moment the complete faith in the
divine origin of his Master, or was this faith also that of the
other Apostles?

It is hard to trace the growth in faith among the Apostles.
There were dark moments in their faith. Look at the indiscreet and shocking action of the mother of James and
John, greatly concerned for the future of her sons. Her sons
had been chosen by the Messiah to be among the twelve
closest collaborators of the future king of Israel! But she
had greater ambitions for them : could they not be his
immediate collaborators, the right and left hands of the
Messiah-King So she goes to find Christ. The two
Apostles, we note, do not oppose this action of their mother.
Jesus replies that she knows not what she is asking for!
Matt. (20. 22–23). And speaking directly to his Apostles,
Jesus says, "Can you drink of the cup that I shall drink
of?" They reply naturally that they can. But did they know,
they too, what that meant?

A short while before the Passion the Apostles asked him
another question : "When will you set up again the
Kingdom of Israel?" And this was only a few days before

Jesus' death. The Apostles grew impatient, they no longer understood : the promised kingdom was not coming! Hence their confusion at the death of the Messiah (Luke 24. 21). Christ never ceased to reject all earthy interpretations of his royalty. And what is surprising is that every time Christ tried to direct the Apostles' faith towards a supernatural and spiritual notion of the Kingdom, they did not understand. It even appears as if sometimes they failed to hear the words of Jesus and let them go.

If there was a constant concern in the thinking of Christ, it was that of the Passion. He knew that he was to die and what would be the tragic and painful circumstances of that death. This thinking was so familiar that he spoke of it on a number of occasions. The gospels give us three of these prophecies in precise terms. He is to be condemned to death, mocked, beaten, nailed to a cross (Matt. 16. 21–23; 17. 22–23; 20. 17–19). The words go in at one ear and out at the other. They retained nothing of it. They could not understand because they could not imagine that it was possible that the Messiah could die. It was inconceivable to them.

All the Jewish traditions affirmed that the Messiah would be a glorious being, a being unlike others, a sort of superman. So the words of Jesus made no sense to them. Further, you know how Peter behaved when he heard this prophecy : "God forbid, Lord. This shall never happen to you!" (Matt. 16. 22). And you know Christ's reaction, for to him it is a temptation : "You are a stumbling block to me, for you are not on the side of God, but of men." Christ knew well that his road would not be an easy road. He knew that he would have to ascend Calvary and suffer agony and death. And this vision was with him all the hours of his life.

Lastly, there was a remarkable characteristic in this : Jesus, even while manifesting himself as Messiah, took it on himself at the same time to hold back in some way the announcement of this declaration, for he knew that people,

because of the ideas they had of the Messiah, would
interpret it falsely. Jesus healed the sick, but he frequently
added, "see that you tell nobody" (Matt. 8. 4 and elsewhere). He sought to resist a current of opinion. This
attitude of Jesus came over clearly in the Transfiguration.
In the West we often fail to measure sufficiently the
importance of this event. The Transfiguration is in the
line of the Jewish apocalypses and of all the traditions
surrounding the messianic expectation and setting out of
the signs which would accompany the coming of the
Messiah in Israel. Among the many signs which were to
mark the manifestation of the Messiah, this was precisely
one – that the Messiah was to appear between Moses and
Elijah. Christ took only three Apostles to go with him
on the mountain, and he was transfigured before them
(Matt. 17. 1–9, etc). It seems that at that moment Christ
wanted to give to Israel a last chance to believe in a
Messiah different from the one they were expecting. For
the messianic sign is radiant : Christ is there, speaking with
Moses and Elijah : no Jew could mistake that. But what
was Jesus saying to the two prophets? Probably he was
speaking of his Passion and death, as the words of Luke
show (9. 31). And yet this sign, so characteristic, seems
reserved to the Apostles alone, and, among them, to those
who had the ability to understand.

This is a remarkable thing. In one way it is so remarkable;
it so struck the imagination and the heart of Peter that he
alluded to it a very long time afterwards, in one of his
epistles (2 Peter 1. 16–18). Thus it is one of the events in
the story of Christ which most deeply marked the three
Apostles who took part in it, even though at the actual
time they were just allowed with their usual weakness and
incapacity to follow Christ at a certain distance. At Gethsemane they became drowsy. It was the same on the Mount
of Transfiguration. They could see only one aspect of the
events.

They received the command of Christ, while they were

coming down from the mountain : "Tell no-one of what you have just seen, until Christ is risen from the dead." Why not? Because if they spoke too openly of this Transfiguration, there would be the danger of starting off again the popular movement which wanted to carry him off to make him king. After the multiplying of the loaves, the people had wanted to do that. In the pain and humiliation of their political situation, the people longed to be set free from Roman colonization, and this explains certain aspects of the treatment of Christ before the Roman Procurator. The title of King of Israel applied to Jesus was an important factor in this.

Christ never ceased to open other perspectives to his disciples, especially his Apostles. They had decided to follow him. But what did that mean precisely? They had faith in their Master, and he told them that he must take up his cross. Christ had not yet been crucified, yet he spoke of the cross to his disciples. The word "cross" was used in Constantinian times as a symbol of glory, as the very sign of Christ's victory. We too have used that word in this way, so that we forget what it meant for the contemporaries of Christ. It meant a brutal and degrading instrument of torture, a punishment, a means of putting to death one who has been sentenced. That was what this word of Christ would conjure up, not only when he spoke of his own death but when as a condition of following him he spoke of taking up the cross, of renouncing self utterly, and of following in his steps. To follow after Jesus meant to live by his word and to carry out his teachings.

I need not remind you what was the state of the Apostles' faith from the moment of Christ's arrest. It is enough to read again the Gospel account.

They were confused. Their faith seemed shaken to its very roots. Had they lost faith in their Master? God alone knows. But what is certain is that everything that happened was unexpected by them and shattered their dreams and their hopes. Listen to the conversation of the disciples on the road to Emmaus : "We had hoped that he was the one to redeem Israel. Yes and besides all this, it is now the third day since this happened! Some of us went to the tomb, and found it just as the women had said, but him they did not see" (Luke 24. 21–24).

All was not simple for them. Some, among them Peter, tried to follow their Master in the Passion. That is one reason why Peter was overcome. It was just because he tried to follow, that he found himself cornered into denying him. Others did not even try. By running away they escaped the temptation. Peter tried to follow. He found himself put to the test – and there he fell! Moreover, the Lord had foretold this. It is remarkable how each Apostle's temperament shows up in the Gospel. Peter is a generous, impulsive type, always ready to talk, believing in his strength. Face to face with facts, he weakened, he was afraid. This was to be seen several times and it underlines again what we noted in the history of Israel, that God chooses human weakness to make clear his power. It was the Apostle who seemed the most versatile, by his perception and his impulsive enthusiasm, that Jesus chose to be the firm rock on which he would build his Church. There seemed to be a sort of contradiction between this role of strength which had to be his and what he was. The name "Cephas", "Peter", did not really seem humanly to fit him. Thus the last conversation between Jesus and his Apostle : "Peter, lovest thou me?" – three times repeated. It came to the point when Peter was deeply hurt. Was it possible that Christ had doubts of his love for him? Jesus wanted to remind him that words were not enough and that faithfulness is a very different thing.

So it was that the Apostles' faith was terribly shaken and purified by the Passion of their Master. It was like a kind of new beginning for each of them. Also they felt themselves more united. They held to one another. They remained faithful to the community which Christ had gathered round him. Soon they would be dispersed, and only on rare occasions would they be together, but they were the Body of Christ and his Church.

The disciples' faith then was purified and renewed by the Resurrection. This is the event which is to give birth to what we call the faith of the Church.

But it is important to consider the manner in which the Resurrection of Christ took place, for it is clear that, according to Christ's intention, his Resurrection was the foundation of faith, even as it was the essential content of it. So Jesus did not wish his Resurrection to be proved, but that it should be believed by his disciples, even the closest ones. First of all it had been predicted a number of times by Christ himself at the same time as he foretold his Passion. He spoke of it also on other occasions, but in parables : such were the sign of Jonas or the Temple which was to be rebuilt in three days.

Then there was the way in which the Resurrection actually happened. There were no witnesses; the only witness was the empty tomb, the shroud lying in a corner, the cords carefully folded up. The first reaction of Mary Magdalene was to think : "They have taken away my Lord and I know not where they have laid him" (John 20. 11–18). Faced with an empty tomb, no one is forced to conclude that the one who was inside had passed from death to life. That they had taken away the body was the most reasonable conclusion.

It was then that Christ manifested himself. But he did it step by step, if I may so put it, and, it seemed to the extent that people believed in him. Mary Magdalene, the first, came to the tomb. She was a woman whose life had been turned upside down by Christ and who had been won by him. She was deeply attached to him, in every part of her being : she loved passionately the one who had transfigured her by freeing her from a life of sin.

And then it was that, deeply shaken by the sight of the empty tomb, she spoke to Christ without recognizing him. She took him for the gardener of the place. "If you have taken him away, tell me where you have put him, and I will come for him." It was remarkable that in this meeting, as also at his appearance at Emmaus, Christ was not recognized at once. It was only when he called her by her name, "Mary", that she recognized him. Jesus, although he had not yet gone up again to his Father's side, was no longer of this world, but of another world. There had to be the eyes of faith to come close to him again and to recognize him.

Finally, there was the wonderful episode of the appearance to the Apostles gathered together (Luke 24. 36–48). Wonderful in the first place because it showed that the Apostles were not ready to believe. They were stupefied, dumbfounded, to the extent that Jesus was obliged to reassure them, and, to prove the reality of his being to them; he asked for something to eat : "It is even I ! Touch me, and take note that a spirit has not flesh and bones, as ye see me have." There was also the attitude of the one who was not there : "Unless I see in his hands the print of nails and place my finger in the mark of the nails, and place my hand in his side, I will not believe" (John 20. 19–29). Christ's reaction was : "Thomas, put your finger here, and see my hands; and put out your hand and place it in my side; do not be faithless but believing." It was always the same : Jesus called for faithfulness in faith. "Because you see me, you believe. Blessed are those who have not seen and yet believe."

Notice how with Jesus Christ faith took on the character of a real engagement of the whole being, in which trust in one person is uniquely important. When I say engagement of the whole being, I mean an engagement of heart and spirit, intelligence and will. When Christ claimed that those who love him are not those who say, "Lord, Lord !" but those who do his will, clearly he was speaking of the engagement of a man in what is most personal : his freedom and his will. This is what response to the call of Christ involves. For the Apostles the meeting with Jesus was the foundation of their faith, and of the engagement of their whole being, even unto death : they came to believe in Christ to the point of being ready to suffer and to die for him. And that, in fact, was what is given to them.

In the Bible the notion of faith appears in its existential and living complexity. Let us remember that its essential elements are also those which define man : intelligence and the heart, knowledge and will.

III

The Contemplative Dimension of the Life of Faith

"Ask and you shall receive, and your joy shall be full"
(John 16. 24)

We live at a time when prayer is undergoing serious questioning. Not only therefore must we ask ourselves what prayer is, but also examine the objections which are made to it. Some say that prayer is an escape from action, that it points to a state of irresponsibility in the Christian and encourages in man an unhealthy sense of his own powerlessness. Others say, for example: what is the use of praying for peace, if we do not do what has to be done to set it up? For it depends entirely on man to make peace. We have to act before praying! Rather than praying, is it not more important to make charity and justice real? Besides, the Lord himself told us the same thing, when he said, "It is not by saying, Lord, Lord, that we enter the Kingdom of heaven, but it is by doing the will of my Father" (Matt. 7. 21).

So we must not hand the responsibility to God by prayer. "They that do the will of my Father": we have then to act, not being content with good intentions, in the heart, nor good words, as the Apostle John says in his epistle (1 John 3. 18).

Further still, does it not often happen that we feel a certain weariness over prayer because we do not see how effective it is? And then we do not always see the bond of cause and effect between prayer and the Christian life. We know numbers of people who pray and, despite that, are far from being stripped of self, who are neither charitable nor upright. On the other hand it happens that we meet men who do not pray, and who are good, upright and charitable. So we ask ourselves if there really is a link between prayer and perfection.

Why pray when we know that the course of the laws of nature will not be interrupted? There are psychological laws, biological laws, physical laws, meteorological laws. Formerly, in dry countries, men prayed to get rain, whereas now they seek technical means to provide irrigation : it is more effective. And when the radio announces drought why say prayers when we know that all the physical conditions are in conformity with the laws of nature? Rather than praying to God in litanies to preserve us from typhoons and earthquakes, ought we not to concentrate on predicting them?

And then, what about contemplative prayer which asks for nothing, is that necessary or indeed is it possible? I am not speaking here only of the normal prayer of Christians but that of men and women, contemplative religious. Why do men and women withdraw from the world to give themselves up to this wholly interior occupation? Has it a meaning? Why sacrifice lives for that when there is so much to be done !

Further, it is true that people sometimes feel a need for solitude, for reflection, a need for what is called "seeking the resources". But does this not encourage us to pray in a void? Does not "seeking the resources" happen infinitely more effectively by communicating with others? Then we are mutually enriched and spiritually strengthened.

Praying today is difficult. Quite apart from anything else there is so little time to pray. Rarely can we do one thing without sacrificing another. Every day we sacrifice something. We never have time to do what we ought to do.

C

So why put aside time for prayer, when we are not convinced of its efficacy? On the other hand some say : "After all, why not pray all the time, and is not action the best of prayers? A charitable action is a prayer, our work well done is prayer. In this way I pray all the time, my whole life is prayer : so all is well!" Many people feel like this, even Christians.

How are we to answer all these objections? It is to Jesus Christ that we must turn. We cannot find the way out without listening to the Son of God, for if we pray, it is as Christians. Of course non-Christians pray, there is prayer to be found in all religions : but as far as we are concerned, it is as Christians that we pray.

Let us first take a look at the Gospel; it teaches us that Jesus prayed. It is remarkable to note that the incarnate Son is seen to be in perpetual dialogue with his Father concerning all that matters about the accomplishment of his mission, especially the Passion, and the purpose for which he has come. The culminating moment of this dialogue is Gethsemane, the prayer of agony in the garden of olives : "Father, if it is possible, let this cup pass from me ! Yet not what I will, but what you will!" (Matt. 26. 39). This is a real prayer, a supplication ! And this prayer had to be spontaneous, drawing on the depth of his soul. Thus, Jesus, the Son, speaks to his Father.

Although it was as Son ever in the presence of his Father and in full dialogue with him, Jesus was no less a man, and what especially concerns us is that he feels the need, in spite of permanent contact with his Father, to get away from the crowd at certain moments, especially those nights which he passed in prayer in desert places.

It is remarkable also that Christ addresses his requests to his Father. Every time he has to do something important Christ prays. He prayed on the mountain before choosing and calling his Apostles to join him in mission. At the moment of naming Peter as the foundation of his Church, he prayed : "I have prayed for you, that your faith fail not" (Luke 22. 32). Saint John, who had more than any other disciple penetrated his Master's prayer life, gives at the end of his gospel, a summary which is called the priestly prayer. It is a vast prayer, a prayer which covers the world and covers the centuries. Jesus prayed for all Christians, he prayed for the Apostles, he prayed for the Church, he prayed for unity, he prayed for peace.

We have another summary, if I can so put it, of the prayer of Christ in the "Our Father". I believe we are to see in this short spoken prayer a reflection of the very prayer of Christ himself. The Apostles, who were simple men and who had not yet been initiated into any other way of prayer than that of the public prayer of the synagogue, were amazed and struck by the prayer of Jesus. So one day, when their Master came down from the mountain, they said to him, "Lord, teach us to pray" (Matt. 11. 1). And Jesus gave them the Our Father. We could say that in these words there is the essential text of the great intentions of the prayer of Christ.

Finally, on the Cross the prayer of the Son of Man became a total offering of himself. Those cries that he made in his agony are spoken to his Father, either to ask of him forgiveness, or to tell his suffering, or to deliver his soul, all his life, into the hands of his Father. Jesus prayed, and Jesus wanted his disciples to pray like him and with him.

The Gospel contains a certain number of teachings of Christ, on prayer. These teachings, as often as not, do not catch the attention of Christians very much. They are in in fact delivered to us in very concrete parables. Those who want to pray are looking more often for practical directives and methods. Those who try to pray without always getting there would like to know the way to get there, and are sometimes, without always admitting it, somewhat deceived by what Christ said in the Gospel about this matter. This is especially true of the calls to perseverance. We must never give up praying, this is stressed. "Ask, and it shall be given; seek and ye shall find; knock, and it shall be opened up unto you" (Matt. 7. 7). It looks as if Christ is teaching us the art of importuning him in prayer.

The prayer of Christ is timeless. Christ ceaselessly intercedes with his Father (Rom. 8. 34; Heb. 7. 25), and this unending prayer is as it were the continual bringing about of the spiritual transformation of humanity, the fruit of the sacrifice offered on Calvary, as the greatest prayer of all; this uninterrupted prayer of the glorified Christ is given to us in the Church.

What is the prayer of the Church?

Christ is first of all present in the heart of each Christian, of each man united to the Church, who can thus pray in Christ and with him. But the sum of all the prayers that men can raise to God does not constitute what is called the prayer of the Church.

Here we must be certain of one aspect of the Church. We cannot think of the Church as the union of all those who believe in Christ; it is not simply a collected body or an assembly.

The Church has a personality of its own, which comes from Christ's presence in her. When Christ speaks of the Church, he speaks of it as of a living body; he compares it also to a tree. It is a matter of real organic unity which goes beyond the actual life of the members. It is this living unity which is the reality of the Church. The words used by Saint Paul are very clear in this sense.

The prayer of the Church is expressed, of course, in the prayer of each Christian. Apart from them, of course, it could not exist. And yet it is a reality which goes further; there is the prayer of Christ and this prayer is present in the Church, in the prayer of worship; and the height of this is in the Eucharist, the living Incarnation of the prayer of Christ.

We can then arrive at this first conclusion: Christ prayed, and the Church would not exist and would not live without this divine and human prayer; the Kingdom of God would not spread without the prayer of Christ.

But the Kingdom of God could not actually be established by force, nor by constraint, for it is a Kingdom of Love. It is a fragile Kingdom breached by sin, by selfishness, and by every injury to freedom of the spirit and the will. This weakness of the Kingdom of God, neither Christ nor God can alter, for it would be in that very act the destruction of man set in the image of God, for this necessitates his freedom. It is just there that we find the prayer of Christ : it is the eternal perspective of the Kingdom; it is there, at the place of meeting of the finite and the infinite, of the freedom of man and the omnipotence of God.

Christ wants us to share in his prayer. Because we are free beings and responsible, Christ treats us as such. It would be too easy for us to say that the prayer of Christ is enough for us, and we have nothing more to do than to gather its fruits, and so to rejoice for being taken up by Christ for ever, to the end of the world !

In the same way that the suffering of Christ only brings about redemption in so far as that human suffering is united to the Cross of Christ, even so the prayer of Christ calls for participation by men. As Saint Paul teaches, the Christian ideal is to be like Christ, for Christ is man in truth, perfect man, the new Adam. Further still, it is Christ henceforth who lives and prays in man, who should experience in himself the very sentiments of Christ. Outside us Christ is living, and he intercedes ceaselessly for us : this prayer of Christ is an actual reality. On the other side we are called to join in this prayer. This is not easy, and we have "to be taught to pray". The special occasion for the joining of our prayer with that of Jesus is clearly the liturgy of the Church. Liturgical prayer is necessarily centred on the Eucharist, for this incarnates the offering of Christ and his intercession in such a way as to make it present, to bring it within the range of our sharing. So liturgical prayer demands from us a total personal engagement.

Sometimes there is a tendency to oppose liturgical prayer

and individual prayer. From what we have just said it is easy to see that this is basically false. Such an opposition could not have meaning; there could be no liturgical prayer without each and all taking part with all his understanding and all his heart. We are not passive participants; liturgy is not like a play that we just sit and look at. There is no prayer of the Church without the prayer of Christians.

Liturgy takes us into the prayer of Christ, but as it does so, it calls for our participation. So we have to learn how to pray. Thus, liturgy is a school of prayer, and it is for the vast majority of Christians the unique place where they learn to meditate on the Word of God and to encounter the Word in the eucharistic action. Hence the importance of liturgy well done and worthily celebrated.

All prayer is personal, this is evident, and so we also have to pray outside the liturgical assembly. This is a need for every Christian, and it has very many forms according to vocations and gifts received : we have always to take account of the two dimensions of man, which are, on the one hand the fact that he is a social being, and on the other his need for intimacy. This double need has to be satisfied for the growth of the personality. There are Christians who have a tendency to avoid some liturgical reform because it upsets customs of prayer which are too individual. There are those of them who do not like to sing, while others prefer a more quiet, more intimate participation in liturgy. There will always be a legitimate diversity in this matter. Those who rejoice too easily in an exterior sharing in the liturgical action need to deepen their prayer in silence, while those who have too individual a concept of prayer will do well to learn the value of prayer which is also brotherly communion, a bringing about of that saying of the Lord : "Where two or three are gathered together in my name, there am I in the midst of them" (Matt. 18. 20).

In the same way that man needs to live in society, he also needs the intimacy of the home : he cannot throw out one or the other of these dimensions without making himself unhappy. A Christian who was content with public prayer, with prayer at meetings or even liturgical prayer, would be a Christian lacking a certain dimension. So we have to understand this intimate and personal prayer and set ourselves to find a place for it in our life.

But before all else we must ask ourselves what prayer is.

Why not take that very simple definition of Father de Foucauld : "Prayer is thinking of God by loving him". Prayer gets love going; there is no prayer without love; nor is there either prayer without a thought which moves out to him who is loved.

Prayer in one way makes real a presence of love. Take for example what happens when you are parted from someone you love. The love you have for that person can carry you to him, even without your actually thinking about him; however when there are at the same time prayer and love, then you really come close to the one you love.

Clearly when it concerns God this can only be done by faith; faith in Christ and through him. But prayer poses its own difficulties. Is prayer a spontaneous act, just like a natural need? Is it the fruit of human feeling, of a deep instinct? There are in fact moments in our life when we should like to go and weep in the lonely shade of a church. At other times when we experience real joy; then we feel the spontaneous need to open ourselves to God.

There are moments in man's life when he feels the need to express these feelings before God. But this is not the usual way, prayer cannot be considered as something natural. Prayer is not a psychological need, it is demanded by faith, it is a demand by our baptism in Christ.

It has been said that prayer is the breath of the soul. But to put it this way implies a notion of easiness and natural-ness which is not the pattern of actual prayer. Neverthe-less it remains true in one sense, that the life of the spirit needs prayer to expand, to oxygenize itself, to attain to its fulness, its profound desire for eternity.

I should like now to go deeper into this idea of prayer,

answering the objections which have been made to it. I shall take them one by one, and, as we look at them, we shall see what truth they contain. That will help us to think more concretely about prayer.

A first objection considers prayer as an escape from responsibility. This can be true in certain cases. Take for example the matter of war. We are told that we must pray that it will come to an end. We pray, we organize vigils to pray for peace, and as we know that God to whom we address our prayer is almighty, we think that by this praying we have done all that can be done for the setting up of peace.

But such an attitude is not necessarily right. What actually is prayer when it is a demand addressed to God? I am taking the example of peace for it is one of the most instructive. Prayer is closely connected with desire : if my desire for peace is not authentic, my prayer is not worth much. We cannot play games with God. He who prays is he who lays before God the intensity of his desire. If I really want peace, if I am sincere and my want is generous, my prayer will be strong, for it will go along with the efforts I shall make to the full extent of my ability, to work effectively to establish peace.

Christians often need this matter explained. When we call for prayers for peace, we do not make it clear enough that this prayer is not authentic if those who pray do not at the same time do all they can to bring about peace, for after all it is man's task to make peace.

It is the intensity and the reality of the desire expressed to God which gives the value to prayer. And we have to carry this out. But then, someone may say, why pray, if peace depends on men and if, as far as I am concerned, I do all I should to establish peace? But then, we might reply, if peace is within the power of men and if most men sincerely want it, why do they not achieve it? They do not succeed, despite their good will, because there is sin, and that is where prayer comes in.

The prayer of mankind finds all its power when it comes together with the prayer of Christ in the light of that mysterious growth of the Kingdom of God in the heart of man. Whatever we do, we know the limitations of our action and its effectiveness. Prayer has to deal with the freedom of men and their egoism, or more often with their weakness and their mistakes. It is not enough to put everything down to sin and the refusal to love. Good will has its limitations and man is constantly making mistakes.

In all human effort there is then a large element of uncertainty, ineffectiveness, and that is where prayer comes in.

In the course of the centuries, this long struggle of human liberty for the establishment of peace, for the fight against injustice, oppression, strife, extreme nationalism cannot finally be settled unless the mysterious action of grace operates in the deeps of human hearts. So this action which is that of the Kingdom of God and of Christ in the depths of the heart, cannot go further without the collaboration of our prayer. Christ depends on our prayer, for he cannot do things without us, because of our freedom.

The participation of Christians in the deep and perpetual prayer of Christ is then necessary so that the Kingdom of God may be established among men.

"Thy kingdom come", that is a dominant part of Christ's prayer. Even Christ himself must pray that men learn to overcome sin and also that they may be enlightened in their plans, for the more complex the task of humanity becomes, the more men have need to be enlightened. Men are weaker than they think.

God waits for the co-operation of our prayer. And that prayer must always be one with the essential intention of the prayer of Jesus which is the establishment of the Kingdom of God, and that cannot be unless man receives from the Spirit of God this help of light, strength and love which he has need of so as to realize it.

Does this mean that we ought not to pray for small things? Take a boy praying for success in his examination.

This is for him, at his start in life, an important matter. But what does this prayer mean? What is its value? If this boy is praying to have the courage to work well, to become stronger, more generous, his prayer goes along with a real effort on his part. We all have the need to pray to be faithful every day. That is where the demand of prayer comes in. But if this boy prays without making any effort and to ask that his examiner sets questions of which he knows the answers, then his prayer has no meaning!

In the same way, to pray for the stability of a home, for an adolescent in moral difficulties, is truly Christian, within the context of faith. All that is the kingdom of prayer because we are feeling the freedom of man's heart.

Monica prayed with tears that her son Augustine might find faith in Christ, so much so that we might reasonably say that Saint Augustine was the son of his mother's tears. This is a point at which the action of men cannot do very much : the depths of the human conscience. It is there that the Kingdom of God is to be found for it is established in the secret of the conscience of men, beyond their ignorance, the lack of awareness and their mistakes.

Others object that the object of the Christian life is love : we shall not be judged by our prayer but by the perfection of our love. True, but prayer is in love, it is itself an act of love.

The point is to know whether I can love perfectly without praying. Can my love for my neighbour and for God be perfect without prayer.

It is right to distinguish prayer from what is called "an exercise of prayer". Prayer looked at in this way is actually secondary, which does not mean that "exercises" of prayer cannot be useful or even necessary. But they are not prayer, even when they are the way or the means of it.

Love is above that, and it is the soul of prayer. Further, prayer is within love, it is conceived as an act of love and in sight of love. According to what we have just said, it is easy to understand how prayer works in making love real;

nothing is more fragile than love, nothing is more dependent on the freedom of men and their weakness, nothing is more subject to the temptations of wealth, of egoism, of power and the disordered instincts of the passions.

But then I may be asked : could we not be content to have this desire for God continually at the bottom of the heart? To desire God is to pray. In this way we should be praying without ceasing and it would no longer be necessary to reserve times for pure prayer. This is a question which deserves to be taken deeper.

I said just now that all prayer presupposes both love and thought together. We must hold firmly on to this concept of prayer. If the Lord gives us the ability to think frequently on him, at the same time that we give ourselves with all our heart to the service of our neighbour or to other tasks, of course we are in a state of prayer. But it is very likely that we will not be able to attain to that state, nor stay in it, without from time to time consecrating moments to God alone in prayer.

This habit of thinking often of God allows Christians continually to offer their life to God, to make of it that sacrifice of which Saint Paul speaks and which is the true goal of Christian perfection.

This is an important aspect of that union with Christ of which the Eucharist is the sign. Sharing in the eucharistic sacrifice can have as its fruit the transformation of ourselves, to the extent that our life can be wholly a sacrifice united with that of Christ. In this transformation we should be actively collaborating, and it is in this way that each eucharistic communion should be a fully responsible sharing in this mystery of death and life. In this way there comes about that interdependance between action and prayer, which enables a Christian to transform his work, his difficulties, his activities whatever they be, into a spiritual gift, a gift made to God and also to his brethren, the one not going without the other.

And then let us not forget that prayer is before all else a

fruit of the Holy Spirit : it is the Holy Spirit who prays in us and helps us to pray.

But the calls of charity urge us sometimes to the point where we do not find time for prayer. The complexity of our duties and activities hems us in and we seem to be caught in a net. Have we a duty to pause in our activities and to make of that interruption an offering of our time to God?

If we take an overall look at the teaching given by God in the Bible, we see that the notion of adoration consists before all else in allowing nothing as equal to God, in not setting up a creature as an absolute, in not letting ourselves build up idols in our lives : "Thou shalt have none other gods but me" (Exodus 20. 3). So we are not to be the slaves of money, or of power, or even of political activity.

But since the coming of Jesus, God is calling for something more, as a personal act of adoration. Does not adoration demand a halt to the ceaseless round of daily life?

The idea of the sabbath is very important. First, God considers it a necessity for man to learn to stop his activities for rest : hence the idea of rest on the sabbath. This rest can take on a sacred meaning, and it is circumscribed with regulations whose end is to rein or interrupt activity, not just work but also almost every other activity.

This calls for thought, for the whole idea of rest is crucial for a balanced life and for the effectiveness of both intellectual and spiritual endeavour.

When we read the prescriptions of Judaism about the sabbath, we are surprised and even shocked to see how far these prescriptions go to halt all human activity : they prevent men from travelling too far by prescribing the distance which they must not exceed; they forbid cooking, so as to free men from household chores. But whatever the good of such legalism, the greatness and essential meaning of sabbath remain. Man has to learn to rule his activities and to prove that he does rule them by knowing how to halt them. In this way he gives a proof of his freedom, and educates his personality; he is master of his own life.

Hence the need for careful thought about the whole question of managing time.

In the observance of the sabbath, this abstention from activity is offered as an act of adoration, it is a recognition of the sovereign domain of God over us and all things. This is the second aspect of the sabbath, the deepest one. We should have the courage and the will to stop our activities, if only for an instant, in homage to God, in order to pray to him in humble adoration.

It is rather unfashionable today to reflect upon the dependence of man on God. But we have to remember that God can and does call for what he knows is right to suit us, even when this contradicts our natural tendencies and our immediate interests.

We must never neglect this study of adoration for by it we enter the adoration given to the Father by Christ, the only perfect adoration, which calls for our participation. This state of prayer into which the Christian has to find his way is a habit he must create little by little so as to train himself to think of God from time to time. The irreplaceable action of the Holy Spirit cannot dispense you from making the effort to pray, from wanting to do so and applying yourself to it with faith and perseverance.

A third objection is that of the ineffectiveness of prayer. We know this so well that we often find ourselves incredulous about some gospel texts. When for example our Lord states: "Whatsoever ye shall ask in my name, I will do" (John 14. 14), and when he adds: "Ask and ye shall receive, and your joy shall be full" (John 16. 24). There are other still more imposing texts: "Truly I say to you, if you have faith and never doubt . . . even if you say to this mountain, 'Be taken up and cast into the sea', it will be done" (Matt. 21. 21; cf. Luke 17. 6).

Some might conclude they have no faith because they dare not tell a mountain to cast itself into the sea, or a fig-

tree to wither, for they know that just will not happen!
Often we pray whole-heartedly without getting what we
ask. Is this lack of faith? I dare not ask for a miracle, so I
have not faith!

I believe the answer to this lies in the purification of
prayer; we have to enter into the prayer of Christ; our
prayer united to that of Jesus is effective, but we cannot
claim it; it is all-powerful, but its realization is spread over
the centuries for the establishment of the Kingdom of God :
it is not our business to seek the immediate realization of
our requests. We are in the darkness of faith and the
patience of hope.

Besides, Christ himself shows us in parables that we have
to be able to wait, or even that the Father will give us something different from that which we ask him for. We are
often like children who do not know what they want.
"What father among you, if his son asks for a loaf, will give
him a stone . . . or if he asks for an egg, will give him a
scorpion?" (Luke 11. 11–13). There exist little white
scorpions, which, when rolled up, look like an egg, and the
child asks for one, thinking that it actually is an egg. You
will not give it to him despite his cries, for you know it is a
scorpion; but he does not know it!

God often gives us something different from what we ask
him for. And that is why in a sense prayer is always granted
and it is legitimate to address even humble requests to God.
But Christians should ask above all for the fulfilment of
essential things : the Kingdom of God, peace, the salvation
of the living and departed. It is especially crucial today that
we turn to these central themes of prayer.

I do not know if you remember an incident in the story
of Saint Theresa of the Holy Child Jesus. She had felt very
keenly her vocation to intercession even before her entry
into Carmel. In her simplicity and with that definiteness
which was so characteristic of her, Theresa wanted to receive
from God a sign to show the effectiveness of her prayer.
You recall the tale : one who was condemned to death was

going to be guillotined and Theresa prayed without cease
for his conversion. Up to the last moment he had refused
to see the chaplain. Then, at the very last moment, he kissed
the crucifix which was offered to him on the scaffold.
Theresa saw in this a sign from the Lord, as a reply to her
request, however indiscreet. But afterwards Theresa would
have no further need for a sign to believe in the all-powerful and universal efficacy of her prayer.

Now we can understand why in the teachings of Christ
about prayer perseverance is continually emphasized. We
must not let ourselves just go on asking; we must knock,
knock without ceasing, and it will be opened. Perhaps you
will have to knock all your life; one day surely it will be
opened, but you do not know just when. The Lord would
not have told us to knock, if, at the first move, it would
be opened to us. Anyone would knock if they knew the door
would open straightaway!

So prayer is not only motivated by our sharing in the
prayer of Christ for the establishment of the Kingdom of
God in the hearts of men, but it is also a normal attitude
of man in his earthly situation. Prayer sets us in that
attitude which alone is fitting before God. A christian who
refused to pray or never gave a thought to prayer would
be implying that he was sufficient unto himself. If we
think we really are sufficient unto ourselves, we feel no
need for prayer. On the other hand if we know we have
need of God, of divine grace, we are already in the attitude
of prayer.

It is fitting to remember here the words of Christ about
how christians should be childlike. The child asks, the
child has no knowledge of being able to do anything by
himself. Face to face with God, face to face with our life
to be lived through to the end with all the temptations and
weaknesses that threaten it, a prey to pride and egoism the
germs of which are in us, how can we afford not to pray?
We cannot trust in our own selves.

Yet we have to have confidence in ourselves, but humbly.

This is no matter of weakness or lack of boldness – on the contrary humility is a very great strength, for it alone lets us act without doubt about ourselves, without fear of deceiving ourselves before others, without fear of being humiliated. We are held back from some course of action by pride, so often by fear of looking ridiculous. Real humility has never weakened anyone; on the contrary, it makes them stronger. This is the implication of the growth of our relationship with God when we pray.

A last difficulty in prayer rises, in our days, from a change in the psychology of men, who do not feel inclined to ask for things which would interrupt natural laws. Such a contingency deeply offends the scientific mind of today.

I have mentioned droughts and earthquakes. How can they be prevented from happening? It is more in conformity, they think, with the dignity of man to look these realities in the face and to be on guard against these disasters, for example by enabling oneself with a better knowledge of geological laws to put people into shelter. That seems the only possible and effective solution. Equally it would be more effective to build houses which do not fall down. As regards fire there are now insurance companies; there are also fire-resisting materials. On the road, one can put in the car a medal of Saint Christopher; one can also, and this is better, take care to avoid stupidities on the road and drink a little less alcohol before taking off! Yet only God is omnipotent. Let us not forget this. The relationship between him and each of us is a relationship of love, even when there seem to be laws of chance and blind fatality which are at work. When it concerns those you love, your children, you do not want them to be victims of an accident. But that does not depend only on the goodness of the children, nor even perhaps on that of others; so we find ourselves back in that mysterious domain we call chance. Yet the mystery stands, and so it would be unreal to think of prayer to God as useless and outworn when praying that we ourselves or those whom we love should be spared from misfortune.

When it is really a question of something that touches you deeply, when it is a matter of serious illness in one of your family, you know that then you have need to pray, to beg, even if it is a miracle you are asking for! And you will be right! Read the Gospel again : why do we not act like the poor folk who came to beg the Lord to heal them? Jesus, far from criticizing them, loved them, and sometimes he gave their faith as an example.

Do not let us stand up with our reason before God. We are in great danger of deceiving ourselves. Scientific advance, the type of mind that it produces and the fact of living in a technological world bring about changes in man, but they leave unchanged the mystery of the ruling of the world by a God who is free and loves all creatures.

This then is a consequence of faith : "Whosoever does not receive the Kingdom of God as a little child, will not enter therein" (Mark 10. 15). That saying no one can ever erase from the Gospel; it forms part of that treasure of life which Jesus has handed on to his disciples and which is ours. True, that childlike openness with God, that simplicity of relations with him, are very strange to the mentality of a materialistic world, and generally speaking to those around us. For the majority of people such a demeanour is meaningless. Yet a Christian has to be logical in his faith and to act in conformity with it. That is what makes the greatness of the saints. A man like Charles de Foucauld lived in utter loyalty to God and to his own Christian being.

Is it reasonable, is it possible, is it within the vocation of every Christian to entertain the possibility on earth of an intimate and personal relationship with God? We have to reply, "Yes", from the very fact of what a Christian is. Every Christian has to know who Christ is, he knows him as the Son of God, he knows that Christ is living and acts in each one of us. Faced with such a reality we are bewildered; we are confused, for we tend to represent God in an anthropomorphic way. We have to purify our idea of God. And yet we can think of God without having to imagine him in a particular way. Here lies the difficulty. We find it hard to believe that God can be interested in each one of the hundreds of millions of men on earth! We imagine it impossible that he should share his attention among millions of beings. We say to ourselves, "I cannot be of any interest to Him!"

So we come to doubting whether we really are loved, for if we are so insignificant, how could we be loved by God? To be loved is something which implies a very close relationship with him who loves.

We are the victims of our own imagination. God is so simple that we cannot understand him. We could as well, if we stick to images, represent God to ourselves as a point infinitely more concentrated than by the picture of the vastness of the cosmos : and these two ways of representation have in neither of them greater truth than the other when it is a question of the divinity. God is such that he cannot share himself out; when he gives himself, it is wholly, and what he gives to one, he does not take away from another. This helps us to understand a number of things better, especially how the heart of Christ is utterly whole for each one of us, as the Passion of Christ is whole for each one, as God is wholly present in the very depths of the spirit of each man, in his heart, in his being, and in all his life. It is a total presence, a total attention to all and to each. God is one and many. In fact God is beyond images! God has no need to be attentive : it is we who are inattentive to his presence.

To come back to contemplation, we might say that it is a supernatural attention to the living presence of God in the depths of our being. How can that be possible? This knowledge is more an experience of God, full of the light of love, an experience which can pour forth from the faith and love which Christ has set in our hearts. This faith and this love are by their very nature adapted to knowing and loving our brethren in Christ. It is the work of the Holy Spirit, who has been sent in order to give us the light and strength of love which is not of this world.

The same Spirit gives us the wisdom which directs our attention; he gives us light so as to make us better understand the Gospel when we read it, and discover therein the authentic face of Christ; he gives us the judgement to decide what is better, and the strength to carry it out. We have to believe, in this life in which we are sharing. When we say together the prayer to the Holy Spirit, let us ask earnestly that this life be given to us in abundance.

There are people who have realized in their life this perfect union with the Lord. Father de Foucauld is one such. It is impossible to read his writings without discovering the extent to which this man has been utterly enraptured by the love of Christ, to the point of feeling the persistent need to go away alone with him into the solitude of the desert : and it was there, in a more intimate union with him, that he discovered a new way of loving men which surpasses all earthly limits.

What I want to emphasize now is the contemplative aspect of his union with God, which took the form of a total presence with Jesus and of a real dialogue with him as the expression of his love. You may say to me that these are exceptional vocations : true, but these exceptional vocations are only a taking to the limit of what every Christian is called upon to live. Every Christian is capable of entering into close relations with Christ; he has the basic aptitude for this, which is more or less developed according to his response, and following up what use he makes of it, for contemplation is, by the grace of God, a reality which can be achieved. There exist a great diversity of vocations, and I am not pretending that you are all called to the same degree of union with the Lord by contemplation. But it is important to realize that you are not of a different race than that of the contemplatives, that you have received the same grace, that they were men like you, Christians like you.

There is in the life of every Christian an indispensable contemplative core. Every Christian possesses the potentiality which this gives and which we see at its fullest in the great contemplatives. Certain of them were also given to us as signs, as an invitation to think seriously on this need of personal contact with Christ and with the invisible world, which is more necessary than ever in our days if the Christian is to rise up to his full stature. The more man finds himself responsible for himself, the more he has to find in himself, in his own life, this intimate contact with Christ; he will have still more need of this as he is less and less protected by the world in which he lives; for we live in a world which is secularized, materialistic, even when it is not explicitly atheistic. I am speaking here of the responsibility of each Christian. We must not confuse psychological understanding with the growth of contemplative prayer which attains mysteriously to the vision of God. That is something quite different.

It is true that psychology has much to teach man as a spiritual being; it demonstrates the need to reflect, the need for silence; it shows the need for deep communication with others, the need to be strengthened by them and to think over together so as to see better how one ought to live. But those moments of solitude with Christ, of intimate union with him, will bring you light that men cannot give you and make you aware of your true personality as sons of God : that is quite different from a spiritual strengthening which one man can give another, although both are necessary, and each calls for the other, for him who lives in the world and wants to go to the limit of the demands of his Christian calling. Contemplation is also a resource, but of a different kind, and one much more essential.

It is at this point, in the relation of action and contemplation, that we understand the basic unity of Christian life. We search for unity in our life and it is a vital need.

But the place of this unity has so to speak two faces. For it is with one same love that we love Christ Jesus, God and our brethren. The unity of this love is fundamental in Christian life; it is of the spiritual order, it is of the supernatural order, and it can only be the work of the Holy Spirit.

We should not go searching for this unity on a purely psychological level. There will always be the need for a rhythm in life, for this is indispensable for any man who wants to use his intellect, who wants to think. We have to accept the necessity of this rhythm and alternate times of solitude and reflection with those devoted to exterior activity. It is according to the same principle that you need, as a Christian, a balance between action, which is charity acting upon the world and mankind, and the moments of prayer and solitude in which is expressed the intimate love which binds you to Christ.

Our prayer has to become a spiritual attitude which is extended into action. But that will only take place if we acquire the habit of keeping moments entirely consecrated to God. No man can dispense himself from this rhythm between action and quiet, between presence to mankind and retreat, between active charity and contemplative prayer.

IV

Faith Confronting the Demands of the World

"Be brave : I have conquered the world."

If we contemplate the living Christ, eternally living, we know that what he was yesterday that he is today and that he will be tomorrow, eternally the same. But the Church in its earthly state travels the whole long road of history and we have to know where it has got to. Is it on the march ahead of humanity so as to lead it, to guide it? Is it at the heart of humanity marching with it and at its pace? Or is it right behind, sometimes getting outdistanced and trying to catch up by short cuts while the world is marching on without it.

I want to begin by looking at the world today, at contemporary man and his psychology, and to try and place faith in relation to these.

In any consideration of the world today it is always necessary to take into account atheistic materialism and the advances of science, for they too address themselves to the fundamental questions concerning the salvation of man, his liberation, his earthly well-being. But from the very start the perspective is different.

Materialists, and, generally, all who do not ascribe human life to God, who do not believe in an after-life, consider these problems solely within a human context. A believer too will face the problems of man's salvation, his liberation and his happiness, but his questioning will be from a different perspective, since he believes in a life beyond death and believes that salvation comes from God. When we are in dialogue or in co-operation with the world, then we have to take care about the way its problems are seen, but we also have to be aware of the fundamental difference of approach. This distinction is crucial.

Before speaking of the problem of the mortality of man and of the nature of his problems, I should like to draw your attention to another danger of today's mentality : the difficulty of thinking in depth about the problems which face us and the ease with which slogans and formulae are taken for truths. We all suffer from this. There are a good many theological slogans and I shall soon be quoting you a certain number of these, for today even theology is not exempt.

Clearly, a slogan has the usefulness of simplifying the answers to problems, at least in appearance. Today we like simplicity, and as there is little time for reading or thinking and as the problems are complex, there is in this a real danger for nothing is more disastrous than over-simplified solutions.

But we must ask ourselves first what modern man is. We are always talking of "modern man" like a new being. But does "modern man" really exist?

Here again let us not simplify the reality ! If we look at the world today, we find we are dealing with a whole variety of peoples with very different mentalities. The peasant of a Siberian kolhoz, an African, an Indian worker do not all conform to a single type of modern man. The agricultural workers of Cuba have little in common, as regards their needs and their psychology, with the militants who rule them. The people of India represent again another type of man, so deeply religious that they are often ready to sacrifice their well-being so as to preserve their religious values. So have we the right to say that modern man exists?

Yes, there is a "modern man". He appears to us as the man of the future. He is a man who has been already imbued by industrial and technological society, by the scientific education which he has received, by the nature of the sociological problems which he has to face. This is the type of man who seems to us to be more and more the man of the future. This is as far as we can see, because no-one can foresee what the future will be.

However it is this type of man we have to examine, for it is he who is posing the real questions for the Church and challenging her faith. But are we dealing with a really new type of man, different from those of earlier generations? I know young people who have a philosophy, an attitude, a mentality extremely different from what we would call typical of modern man. There are students in philosophy who are neither marxists nor materialists. Already their reactions, their mentalities are very different. More so perhaps than in days gone by.

We must not let ourselves off lightly by taking the easy line of too swift and too superficial categorizations. Modern man has, deep down, been fashioned, modelled by the world he lives in, by its demands, by its problems, by its culture, by its industrialization. Must we then conclude than man is so conditioned by his environment that he cannot dominate it or affirm his freedom? This is the marxist point of view, according to which man is the product of his environment.

There is certainly an element of truth in this, but we must not lose sight of the fact that man can and also should make himself, and that he should remain free to react to the conditioning imposed on him by his economic or social milieu.

For the conditioning does exist. There are the "slogans" of environment, of money, of sex, a view of life. And, without suspecting it, men are conditioned by all that. The essential question for the Christian will be to learn how to live freely and how to react to meeting what is around him in conformity with the demands of his faith. The present leading ideologies claim to be fashioning a new type of man. This organized effort is especially evident in countries with a socialist regime. Face to face with these views of man we have to work out how to know if, as Christians, we have not to fashion a type of man of whom Jesus Christ is the prototype. But, you will say, how can one take Jesus as a model? But in this lies the task of christianity. It is not easy to map it out, and yet it must be the goal of all christian effort.

Modern man is first of all a man who has discovered the meaning of his dignity and of his responsibility as regards himself and his evolution, as well as regards the evolution of the universe. This new attitude sets man in a situation of conflict with the Church. Actually, until our times, the Church has been, through the ages, the mistress of humanity in a number of domains of culture and civilization. Moreover it still remains so in some countries. The Church has been inextricably bound up with the origin of western civilization, and it kept, in the middle ages, a monopoly in the field of education. This is not the place to give you a history lesson, but this fact makes clear a number of things in the situation of today. The Church has really been the tutor of man, who was like a subject under its direction.

The emancipation of man is the fruit of normal evolution, and it is progressive. But we are not to conclude that in the past man found himself frustrated and was in error. If we had been alive at that period, we should undoubtedly have acted like the men of that period. The Church had to play its part in history. It could not have done otherwise. Change came about very slowly; the Church still carries in it the vestiges of that past, which is something that makes its situation in the world both difficult and serious.

All that has been and is still going on in our days is then something relatively new for the Church. These difficulties are not limited to the Church. They affect all the great religions. Islam, for example, has played a similar role in the Arab lands and has given birth to a whole civilization. In India we find the same situation, whether for Hinduism or for Buddhism.

During a whole period of the history of humanity, the religions have been a determining factor and, as it were, the guide for social development and human culture. It is probably the Catholic Church which feels most strongly the results of this emancipation of man.

What are the consequences for the Church of this emancipation of man and of the secularization of society which is its logical consequence? Fully conscious of its supernatural end and the adaptations necessary, the Church goes through a period of transition, of being rooted up, during which it has progressively and with difficulty to renounce the guardianship which it has in certain domains. On the other hand, man, and especially the faithful, have to make proof of their independence. This spirit of independence, when we find it in the temporal domain, offers no problems; but it extends into the interior of the Church. A tendency to democracy and to a complete autonomy of judgement grows in the Church. The knowledge that each one has the right to decide with full freedom and responsibility his own problems characterizes more and more the mentality of Christians today. They do not address themselves to the question of the fundamental nature of the Church, which to them is then just one society like any other.

There has also been a transformation of the meaning of God amongst most people, not least among believers. They say that the action of God is continuous – that the idea of a Father-God, Almighty, Lawgiver, Judge has to be abandoned – man has come of age. The theology called the "death of God" gives shape in the outcome of this. This theology has something important to say in its claim that the language we use about God is inadequate and that there is a continual need for the purification of the ideas and language we use when we speak of the ineffable. But this is not new – it has always been maintained by the majority of the great theologians and mystics. In the context of today's scientific mentality what is dangerous is that such a theory often leads to an agnosticism, which raises doubts about the very meaning of the Incarnation of the Word in Jesus Christ. Some come, as in a recent book called "God is dead in Jesus Christ", to oppose the traditional idea of God, the Trinity with that of a God who is the source of life and love to be seen in man. What is affirmed is not always false, but what is false is the opposition they claim to set up between this notion of the divinity and the God of Jesus Christ which the Church and her tradition offer to us.

In the theological process we are describing we can discern a kind of dialectic – a reaction sets in to a theological belief which in turn leads to the accepting of new values; these often represent a move forward, a deepening, without necessarily rejecting these beliefs which are the result of centuries of man's experience of God. To me it would be impossible to renounce God the Father, the God Almighty of our profession of faith. But this does not mean that a deepening of these ideas is impossible and undesirable. It would be more accurate to say, in the case we are interested in, that God did not die in Jesus Christ, but that Jesus Christ in dying manifested an aspect as yet unknown of God who is Love, who saves us and manifests himself in Christ. We still have countless ways in which we need to go deeper into the mystery of the revelation of God who is Love, and all the consequences which flow from it in our personal life, for humanity and for the people of God.

Following the basic need for freedom and responsibility which the Church stands for, we can see how crucial becomes a rediscovery of the importance of the interior action of the Holy Spirit. I should say simply that we cannot forget the charismatic action of the Spirit which flows particularly in those whom Christ has made pastors of his Church so as to guide and deepen the faith of God's people.

Man, thus freed in the feeling of his responsibility and his liberty, discovers more and more strongly the true meaning of the demands of the law of Love and this transcends institutions, laws, and precepts – it is the essence of christianity. The belief that all is summed up in the law of Love, sets man in tension even with the divine law, and in consequence starts him questioning the very meaning of sin, the need for self-discipline, and in this dissolves the sense of bearing one's cross and self-sacrifice. All these now find their true meaning.

Human progress continually unfolds new human needs and these must be taken into account. But this has to be done without denying what of the past is true and good, and there lies the difficulty! In the Church, the living body created by Christ, the unity of its biological structure, to borrow a current analogy, is expressed in the Church's tradition. This must not be forgotten.

It is strange how the desire to democratize the Church, to emphasize individual responsibility, and freedom within the Church, comes at the time when ideologies of all sorts and especially marxism are becoming increasingly institutionalized and parties and regimes are demanding from members strict discipline and conformity of the individual to the general will. Recent examples have shown us how totalitarian are the demands of orthodoxy and what little respect they have for intellectual freedom in most of the regimes run by ideologies. Respect for truth, which is clearly an aspect of respect for man, obliges the Church and its members to seek out what is true and good and to hold on to it, however much we may question human values. Without this care for truth there could not be real human freedom.

A second characteristic of modern man is his orientation towards the future rather than the past. We always talk of our projects and the prospects for the future. The past has no further interest apart from its being in some measure necessary to help the working out of our plans for the future.

The young have a certain disdain for tradition, for some this even develops into a kind of hatred for all that tradition represents. All this is understandable. One gets the impression that humanity progresses by stages which are punctuated by breaks in continuity. And yet each time men do not just start again from scratch, but enriched, often without knowing it, by what the past has given them. The sciences have moved forward by the handing down of learning from one generation of scholars to the next. Certain things which are handed down are definite, and any scientist knows how much he owes to the past.

Let me give another example. A Soviet citizen today has inherited in his socialism all the accumulated virtues of a christianity deeply lived out in the past. This struck me when I went to Russia. I spent a day with a party member who took us to visit the ancient churches of his city. There were two men in him – the marxist and the inheritor of centuries of Christian civilization. A man cannot make a total break with the past – it is humanly impossible. Men are the sons of their fathers, even when they deny them.

Nevertheless, as I have said, we live in a time when many are in revolt against the past, or at the very least, they reject the moral principles, the conventions, and *mœurs* of society. Confronted with this how does the Church react? Is she like a great lady, benign but hopelessly encumbered with outworn clothing? Yes, perhaps, a little! In these days we worship progress and give little value to what is changeless. This is particularly true among intellectuals. What does not move, does not evolve. What was true a century ago cannot any longer be accepted as such today. That a system of thinking was thought valuable some years ago is enough to prove that now it is of no value, that it is worn out. This is the judgement of the younger generation and this is why we can understand the figure the Church cuts in the world today.

The Church on the other hand has always had a tendency to look towards the past. It looks conservative, perhaps because it has a feeling of having something to preserve, the tradition it has received from the past. But we must consider the Church carefully, because it has the right to be understood for what it is. If you are a member of the Church, such a thing is incumbent upon you.

A short time before the opening of Vatican II, a well-known theologian gave a lecture on the Church, and I remember he compared the Church to "a lady walking through history with eyes before and behind". This image was not his own invention; he was quoting some writer of the middle ages. The Church has eyes behind because it is obliged to look ceaselessly at that point in history at which she received in Jesus Christ the full revelation of God; and it has eyes ahead because it has unendingly to go forward towards the future, towards the realization of its hopes, but without losing the direction it receives from its roots in the past.

We cannot alter the fact that Jesus Christ was born about two thousand years ago, and that the Revelation of the Father which he made to us, as well as his life and the death on the cross, are events of the past. (I am speaking of course of the events as they appear in history and not in an existential sense.) For Jesus Risen is as young today as two thousand years ago. Moreover the books that hand down the Revelation are a number of documents coming from different periods, they are not modern books.

How then could the Church not look back ! The fact that she does however puts her in a very difficult position. One modern author was able to express what a number of people think about the Church today and about revealed religion in general. Here is what he wrote :

"I am incapable of taking seriously a revelation which was supposed to have been given to our ancestors in time past. I can only believe in those things which the intelligence can grasp and which can be expressed in a way which makes sense to men today. And this in the context of the findings of science, free thought. I cannot believe in the truths of the past, the only truth in which I believe is revealed gradually, grudgingly, daily, imperceptibly more and more."

This represents fairly enough the mentality of many of our contemporaries. And yet Jesus spoke in historic time. This attitude implies not only the rejection of our concept of revelation but even transmissible truth. No truth is forever self-evident; each has to be made now, gradually, painstakingly by each individual. So in this concept of truth there is both a confusion between the different orders of knowledge, and also a rejection of any knowledge not directly based on the experience of phenomena. We cannot go into all this but you ought to be aware of this problem. You cannot understand the nature of your faith if you do not accept a difference to exist between positive sciences on the one hand and knowledge of a metaphysical order on the other. To the latter belong the truths of religion. The fact that the truths of religion abide, expressible and transmissible by intellect, does not prevent the need for the Church to be constantly renewed.

The situation of the Church is then a difficult one. It is natural for the Church to be somewhat conservative over against the volatility of men, at least, if we attribute no importance to the transmission of truths, and only expect the Church to minister to the spiritual needs of her members. But would such a Church be the Church of Jesus Christ? And what would faith in the Son of God mean then?

There is another difficulty for the Church : she has to be the Church of all men without exception. She has to enfold and treat as son every christian of good will who sincerely seeks to be faithful to Christ and to be saved by him. Regardless of differences and of worldly or political convictions, even mutually opposed, poor and rich, young and old, all belong to the Church. God alone judges the hearts of men. No community, no group of men can claim, because of their opinions or even in the name of the demands of the Gospel, to represent the Church, or belong to it in a special way, or to shut out from it those who do not think as they do.

In the first chapter of Father Daniélou's book : "Prayer, a political problem", the author begins by discussing two concepts held of the Church. Some people would like a church of the "pure" – a church made up of christians courageously putting all the gospel demands into practice, especially that of poverty. Others think rather of a church made up of poor, wretched sinners humbly seeking the sacraments and salvation. The Church doubtless has this double vocation but it remains a Church of sinners, a Church of the poor, the Church of all. She has to be the Church of christians of all nations – whatever their particular bias; she is the Church of all Brazilian christians, the Church of the Cubans, the Church of all the christians of the world : the mother of all.

It is good for us to remember that the real mission of the Church is to offer and win eternal salvation for all. That is why its problems are different from any others. True, the Church in her notion of salvation does include this striving for the temporal liberation of the poor; all christians have a duty to dedicate themselves to this. But we must not forget that the essential aim for the Church is liberation from sin and that all is set in a perspective of eternity.

Hence the difficulties that the Church finds in adapting herself to new conditions. The Church, being a continually developing society, cannot make a clean break with the past. In the temporal and political order, as we often see today, it is perfectly feasible to change a form of government overnight by revolutionary means or by coup d'état. In human society, it is possible to advance by making a clean break. Indeed, this is perhaps one of the laws of historical development. But things do not work like this for the Church, since she is a living body whose members are living souls. And in any case, at her deepest structural levels, the Church cannot be revolutionized. You can level any number of complaints against her; as far as her membership is concerned, she is full of shortcomings, and like all historical institutions, she is slow to change. She has her monuments, her uniforms, her officers, she has many features carried over from past forms of government. All this is true, and all this could and should change.

We may desire these changes, we can and should help to bring them about. But we must do this in a spirit of love, since for the faithful these are mere appearances, not the true and transcendent nature of the Church herself. A Christian truly believing in the Church should know how to distinguish between the transitory and the abiding.

Make no mistake : even were all these outward and controversial aspects to be changed, the Church would still offer us a trial of faith. The Church would always cause suffering ; Christians would therefore be wiser to remember that they themselves are the Church and that the renewal for which we are all waiting will never come except at the cost of our own patient and persevering efforts.

Modern man looks to the future. Is the Church orientated towards the future? and if so, how? We have seen how the Church is rooted in the past; she is however entirely orientated towards the future. And this is so because her final fulfilment will be as the glorious, perfected Church of the Resurrection. The final perfecting of the Church is nothing other than the final perfecting of every one of her members. But the Church also has the mission of showing men how to establish the Kingdom of God on earth, here and now. Christ is alive, and the Church

E

to which he is so intimately joined and which he quickens from within, is never old – not even when she looks as if she is. Christ's eternal youth is everywhere, concealed behind the out-dated externals. The invisible part of the Church is forever young and up-to-date, though what is visible be marked by the frailty and natural limitations of man. This is the way things are.

For instance, think what a long time it has taken to change the liturgy process, not complete even now. Changes on such a scale have never been undertaken before at such speed. Renovating the age-old structure of Christian prayer has not proved as simple as some people thought it would. Admittedly, several liturgical prayers no longer corresponded to present attitudes, and some of them had actually become offensive to the Christian conscience. Yet, see how important the psalms still are in the prayer of the Church. The psalms are what you might call a primitive cry from the heart of humanity. True, there are cries for vengeance in the Psalter. And this may seem surprising at first. But if we were to go round the world, investigating the hearts and consciences of men, I think that we should find every one of the psalmists' feelings exemplified somewhere or other. And certainly the cries for vengeance! Men are always crying for that. It is very mysterious, isn't it, that these poems, composed so many centuries before Jesus Christ, and expressing the prayers of men at a relatively primitive stage of cultural development, should have become the vehicle for human prayer for so many centuries and have been adopted by the Church for her official offices.

We should do well to think on these things, even if they shock our sensibilities. God is not afraid of man, who is what he is – as though naked – before him. If we use the psalms as our prayer, looking to find our own feelings, our own needs reflected in them, we shall be disappointed. Not so, if we hold the conviction that by means of the psalms – which are the prayer of the Church – the cry of humanity itself rises from our lips. How this will widen our spiritual horizons!

Whether it be in the liturgy or in other domains, many changes will have to be effected in the Church, but not too fast. Is that one of the Church's weaknesses, or a strength, do you think? Whatever the answer, the Church, being rooted in Christ, cannot make revolutionary breaks with her own development.

A third characteristic of modern man is his tendency to universality. The proletarian revolution is represented as an international revolution. Now, what we actually observe in the world today are two virtually opposing tendencies. On the one hand, a march towards unity, confused admittedly : man in his uneasy predicament feels that unity alone holds the key to proper fulfilment of human destiny. And on the other, all sorts of regionalistic, nationalistic and linguistic movements, erupting and crystallizing often enough in violent revolt, expressing an instinctive reaction against a unification of mankind and the standardizing of culture and personality. Never in history have the contradictory tendencies manifested themselves more markedly.

Despite the conflict, mankind is bent on this quest for unity. It seems essential, the only way to world peace. And this naturally highlights the scandal – for many people see it as such – caused by the diversity of religions in the world. As believers, we too must ask ourselves why there should be so many religions. Couldn't unity be achieved in the religious sphere as well as in the political? There are a great many different religions. They bear witness to a general quest for the absolute, and embody the universal human conviction that life continues after death.

Even before God first called Abraham, from whose seed to raise a people who in the fulness of time would give birth to Christ, there were many religions. There were almost as many gods as there were nations. Most of the major religions of the world, from these or similiar origins, have developed alongside the Jewish and later christian religions. We may ask why God did not choose other means to procure the speedier extension of his Church throughout the world. This is difficult ground. We come up against the mystery of human history, and its infiltration by the history of revelation and of salvation by Christ. Jesus, his extra-lucidity of mind notwithstanding, himself blenched at the immensity of the Creator's project. Have you ever seriously considered the true force of Christ's temptations in the wilderness, when he was about to undertake his public ministry? Establishing the Kingdom of God throughout the world – had he the strength to do that? And the temptation he felt was to impose the Kingdom by conquest – spiritual conquest, naturally – on the kingdoms of the world. But in place of this spiritual conquest, what the Father was offering was the Cross. And from the Cross, that hard and cruel way of love – the Kingdom of God must spring. The Church must make her way through this proliferation of religions, in humility, by simple force of love.

So what, in God's plan, is the point of all these other religions? They all witness to the search for God, to a search that precedes any revelation, a hesitant search, though one never in vain. Their affirmation of an otherworldly absolute, their efforts to go beyond self and created things, their great-hearted search for perfection, their genuine moral preoccupations, their respect and love for others : these qualities, all characteristic of the major religions, all contribute to the sum of human welfare. We understand this better than in the old days.

But even within Christendom itself, where a certain universality has been achieved, there have been reactions, unity has been lost from time to time, giving rise to heresies and schisms. But consider, even while that has been going on, there has been a continuous deepening of the religious sense, and the very notion of salvation has taken on clearer meaning. In the times of Saint Francis-Xavier, for instance, it was still commonly held that no one who died unbaptized could be saved. The axiom : *Nulla Salus extra Ecclesiâ* was applied inflexibly and literally. And although this attitude, as we now see, left much to be desired, it did in fact immensely stimulate the missionary movement of the day, giving rise not only to the founding of new churches in foreign lands, but also to a full-scale Operation *Salvation* "to prevent souls from falling into Hell" – as a daily prayer of one of the Missionary Institutions used to have it.

The Church's opposition to some of the indigenous ceremonies of China and India also came from this same conviction that whatever was not Christian was not good. A glance into the past shows us how far we have come since, in reaching a better understanding of what is meant by "saving the heathen". Vatican II was very precise on this matter.

But here another question arises. If indeed the non-Christian religions, above all the great religions such as Islam and Buddhism, contain sufficient qualities for an upright and great-hearted man to find God and be saved, what is the point of missionary endeavour? Isn't it the case that conversion to the Church often puts new Christians in a very difficult position? Once cut off by their conversion from their natural and traditional environment and the moral support that this affords, don't converts often find themselves in conditions less favourable to their ultimate salvation than before they embraced Christianity?

And so we see the need for deeper consideration, before we can understand certain aspects of the Church's role in the modern world. How does the need for unity make itself felt, between the world-religions themselves, as between the various Christian sects? And naturally, within these religions themselves there are differing views on how to resolve the problem of their own internal and optional differences : which too are an affront to the conscience.

The view is held, above all in Hinduism and among certain Moslem sects, that all religions are relative, in the sense that each represents an approach to a centre, which none in fact attains, but on which all converge, as the radii of a circle converge on the centre. The points on the circumference from which the radii begin may be immensely distant from one another; nonetheless the radii grow nearer to each other, the nearer each comes to the centre, at which point they will all be fused into a unity. Thus, the various religions are different ways, all equally valid, to the same end, which is none other than God in his absolute and incomprehensible truth. This syncretic attitude necessarily implies the relativity of dogma. Hinduism in particular takes this view. If you go to the banks of the Ganges, to Benares, and preach the gospel of Jesus Christ, you will have a respectful and attentive audience. Jesus, for most Hindus, is one of the many manifestations of God, like Buddha and Mohammed, like others now and more to come. But once you declare Jesus Christ to be the Son of God and unique Saviour, they will refuse to follow you and no one will listen any more. They have not grasped one particular truth about God, and their syncretic attitude, seductive as it may appear, leads to scepticism and perpetual dissatisfaction.

You can observe the same attitude among the devotees of Caodai in Vietnam. Their religious institutions are of fairly recent date. They hold that God manifests himself and indeed incarnates himself in men of genius on earth. On their temples, statues of Jesus, of the Sacred Heart and of the Blessed Virgin rub shoulders with those of Buddha and even Victor Hugo. This approach to religion has much in common with modern attitudes of mind, with their tendency to abolish dogmatic distinctions to effect the union of all mankind in love. Our contemporaries, with their compulsion to play down the importance of what can be defined and grasped intellectually in favour of what can be lived and experienced, are unaware of the serious consequences that such an attitude can produce, not only as regards faith in Christ, the Son of God and Saviour, but as regards the dignity of man – created to know Truth.

Recently when I was discussing ecumenism with Brother Roger Schutz at Taizé, he said that if speedy steps were not taken to achieve unity, the young would end up by rejecting any idea of Church as such, seeing the churches as no better than obstacles preventing reunion from taking place. The Protestant young are no longer remotely interested in the doctrinal distinctions that originally gave birth to the host of rival sects and churches. The mere fact that these doctrines gave rise to divisions – they hold – voids them of all fruitful significance. Inter-communion is what the young want, and want it passionately – Catholic and Protestant young alike. What are we to think about that?

I should like you to think very seriously about it. If the only thing that matters is love, and if the only content of the Christian revelation is that we should love one another as brothers, should we not be right to let the rest go by the board? If everyone were to unite in the same quest for love, all the doctrinal differences dividing the Protestant sects from each other, and Catholicism from Orthodoxy and the Reformed Churches, would seem empty and meaningless : and there would be one Christianity, united in love for love.

This sort of attitude corresponds exactly to the modern temperament, with its hunger for immediate results and its insistence on only those ideas that can subserve its immediate endeavours. If truth serves to produce an instant result, then it is true. But in such a context, intercommunion immediately loses a dimension as essential to it, as it is to a right view of the Church herself. If the context of faith in the reality of the Eucharistic Sacrament no longer matters, the Eucharistic celebration is reduced to a merely symbolic action, susceptible of any interpretation you may care to give it. In such a context, why not – to be logical – admit even non-Christians to the Sacrament? The very terms in which such questions are couched today should make us realize that the diversity of solutions offered is conditioned by the diversity of philosophies now current, and more particularly by the various notions of truth and of man's ability to know it. In one view, in the ultimate analysis, religion would be no more than a concatenation of feelings and ceremonies to produce a practical effect, the whole based on a purely subjective relationship with an unknowable God. Here the word transcendent is to be interpreted as unknowable. However, if there is indeed a reality, if this reality is true, if it can in fact be grasped by the intellect, and if God is the supreme truth and hence the Supremely Intelligible, then the case is very different.

You have what you might call practical activism, or better still the quest at all costs for results, and this implies a materialistic view of the world. Here, there are no spiritual realities for man to communicate with, given the type of intellect he has. In such a context, fidelity to a doctrine held for true makes no sense. Dogmas are provisional formulations, useful for guiding conduct and for conferring a kind of mystical dimension to our life – a mysticism, however, entirely subjective and relative. And God moreover being unknowable and entirely beyond the grasp of the human mind, it doesn't make much difference what Christians or Moslems or Buddhists may think about him – all their ideas being equally valid and equally provisional. What becomes of the God of Abraham, of Moses and of Jesus, in all this? – a divine manifestation for our benefit, but of a God who never truly reveals himself.

Problems of such delicacy and complexity should be approached with humility and experience. We must be really aware of what is at stake, and of what would happen were the Church to abdicate her position as mistress of revealed truth. We must not jib at this title; it denotes a function explicitly conferred on the Church by Christ. If we think that love is the most important quality for mankind and everyman – as Saint Paul teaches, that charity is above all things – we must not at the same time forget that love cannot subsist without faith and hope. Charity would be no charity, were in not rooted in truth. Love is not some blind, emotional instinct. What would love be, were it divorced from the food of man, his destiny, the purpose of his life, of his suffering and of his death?

Would charity be what it is, had it not both source and end in the living, resurrected Christ, who shows us that God is love? This is not one more simple, relative dogmatic statement, the absolute meaning of which eludes us. For the quality, the density, the fulness of love, of which man is capable, could not exist, were this love itself not the flowering in us of God, of Jesus Christ. Truth, then, is just as indispensable to man as love.

We only have to look around us, or to open our history-books, for us to see how the errors inherent in ideological and political systems inflict more harm on mankind than any lack of love. As Christians, we have a view of man and his destiny, conditioned by the content of our Christian faith and Christian hope; for us, therefore, the demands of love cannot be the same as for those who think that a human being is totally and finally destroyed by dying. For us, man is a being that lives forever. The way we love, therefore, is profoundly conditioned by our hope, entailing a quite different view of earthly things, of the purposes that they should serve, and indeed of human happiness. Our conception of man affects our view of economics and of politics.

For instance : we believe in the importance of truth in the Church. Are we talking of a static truth, or of a living and therefore developing one? The notion of static truth is repugnant to modern man. But a living truth does not mean a relative one. We mean a truth, constantly increasing in scope though ever in the same direction, as we might dig a well down towards the water, always in the same direction, deeper and ever deeper. Now, what is grasped by the intellect as true at one moment in history but is later discarded, is not living truth, but successive truths. In all religions, there are elements : ceremonies, customs, certain moral attitudes, certain laws, that can change and be replaced by others. But if, underlying these exterior practices, there is no doctrine, no living truth, no religion would be able to renew itself or adapt itself, without the risk of completely losing its identity and of coming to an end. All the major religions are aware of this. Islam is going through a crisis of adaptation, so is orthodox Judaism in Israel, so is Hinduism. The difficulties that these religions have in adapting themselves to the modern world and to the rising generations are very striking. And the adaptation cannot be effected unless based on a spiritual content and body of doctrine recognized as true. Without this inner conviction, no religion can adapt itself or develop and still remain itself. We all know the rigour with which orthodox Judaism has been handed down and maintained by the rabbis, and is still practised by the ortho- dox section of the population in Israel; and we know that this is embodied in a collection of legal regulations, very alien to the modern world. Hence, many aspects of modern life are regarded as contrary to the Law. Sabbath obser- vance is severe. On the Sabbath, you must not switch the electric light on or off; you must not even use your car, for fear of producing a spark from the sparking plugs. This is how they go on, on orthodox kibbutzes. But young people have no patience with this sort of legalism, rightly regard- ing it as completely irrelevant to the genuine practice of religion.

Now, the difficulty for these young Jews, athirst for God, is that outside this extremely formalistic Judaism called orthodox, there is still no organized alternative capable of requickening the great Jewish tradition and of responding to their needs.

And Islam offers a very similar situation. Islam has in- herited a strong faith in the God of Abraham, a faith both lively still and deeply rooted. But to this are added what are known as the "Pillars of Islam", that is to say, the profession of faith, prayers five times a day, the Ramadan fast, pilgrimage and almsgiving. Of these practices, some are beyond the reach of some people, as for instance the pilgrimage to Mecca; while others, as for instance the Ramadan fast and to some extent the five prescribed times for prayer, are very hard to fit into the modern rhythm of life. That goes too for the interdiction on all fermented liquor. These ancient practices are now therefore observed by some and not observed by others, and the subsequent heart-searching has produced a deep religious uneasiness. Young Muslims therefore, who have not succeeded in discovering spiritual and moral values, and a sense of prayer and adoration in their religion, run the risk of losing all religious faith, once they find themselves forced by circumstances to abandon these practices.

So we may say that in all religion worthy of the name there is a living truth which, merely because it is living, allows for adaptation and renewal of liturgy and practice. You are aware of the reactions of some Christians, particularly in country districts, when the regulations governing the Eucharistic fast were changed; they thought that religion itself had changed and were naturally very troubled as a result. Similarly, over the changes in the liturgy, particularly those concerning the Mass. And this is where the weaknesses of a superficial religious conviction begin to show. No religion can be universal without the awareness of a living truth, maintaining an unchanging identity through all adaptations dictated by culture, or by situation or by mentality however diverse. And the faithful must be clearly aware of those values in their religion which cannot change and of those other values that can.

The more abstract a piece of knowledge is, the more universal it can become. For example, a mathematical equation is the same for a Chinaman, an Indian, for a European or for an American. Conversely, whatever effects the emotions, or the means of expression, as for instance, liturgy, forms of piety, language, singing, all this can and should change, very radically in some environments. The way Christ is depicted, for instance, which rightly has so important a place in popular devotion, has in fact long since been the monopoly of western painters : as a result, Christ's portrait has been diffused throughout the world in ways that leave much to be desired.

Faced with the problems peculiar to the modern world, we must never lose sight of the fact that our faith is rooted in the word of Jesus Christ. He it is who reveals God to us, reveals God's project of salvation for us. What we ourselves know to be true, whatever happens, that we can never renounce. Faith and objectivity are one.

In conclusion, let me quote a few words by Father Congar. There is a trend in modern theology, known as the theology of the Death of God, which envisages the abolition of the idea of a "God as such" and of a "Church as such" in favour of a relative concept of "a God for others" and of "a Church at the service of man". Now, if this concept contains an element of truth, this very truth presupposes the notion of a God as such and of the Church of Jesus Christ. This is what Father Congar has to say on the subject :

"By refusing to speak of 'a God as such', that is to say, of a transcendent God and of a living Jesus Christ, we end by forgetting, or even by denying, the existence of God and of the Church. The Church is not merely a service existing in the world; she is the product of many divine, hence supernatural acts, which cannot be scaled down to the creation as such, or to world-trends as such.

In a word, we are in danger of neglecting this transcendent aspect, when we try to scale ourselves down to a Church in man, for man, with man, existing within the structures of the world uniquely devoted to the service of the human brotherhood, and no longer the Church of supernatural salvation in Jesus Christ in life eternal."

Once again therefore, I emphasize these two aspects of the knowledge of God and of the Church. And we shall be all the better equipped to meet the modern world, if our faith remains firmly rooted, and roots itself ever more firmly in Jesus Christ, in God the Father revealed to us by Christ, and in the Church which Christ divinely founded.

V

Faith in the Bread of Life

"Whoever eats me will draw life from me."

The Eucharist is a baffling mystery for human reason. When we consider that uninterruptedly, throughout the entire Christian Church, for the last two thousand years, bread and wine have been consecrated and offered as the Saviour commanded in memory of him, we are not faced with an abstraction but with a prodigiously concrete reality : the reality of bread and wine. What Christ intended, by founding, by creating, the Eucharist, he and he alone can tell us.

What Christ himself did on the eve of his death, and what has been done since, over and over again, innumerable times, by virtue of the power that he himself conferred, is truly one and the same thing. Whether done by Jesus, or by the priests instituted by him, it is always the same Eucharist, it always will be the same. It will endure century after century, until the end of the world.

The type of bread may change, the type of wine may change, the accompanying prayers may change, but the words pronounced by Christ will not change, and the Eucharist will be what Christ made it; men have no power over it; no one can debase it.

Here then we find a very clear, a very concrete reality, which we can see, which we can touch, which we can eat, but the true nature of which we can only grasp by faith in the words of Christ. This then is a true example of what faith is, since nothing is visible to the eye, nothing is verifiable by experiment, everything is of the order of the invisible. It is a reality which faith alone can reveal to us. Were we to run through the history of the varying forms of Eucharistic celebration, or of the endless speculations of Catholic or non-Catholic theologians who have attempted to understand and define what the Eucharist is, this would fall short of the necessary act of faith and we should none of us be any the wiser. So I shall write no theological study now, but merely an account of what a Christian ought to believe about the Eucharist.

We know that we cannot change either Christ's words or the reality that he has created : this has been the faith as held by the Church since earliest times, and it is true.

You are familiar with the Gospel account of how the Eucharist was instituted. It occurred a few hours before Christ died. The Eucharist is immediately linked to the Passion. And this is one of the first things to be understood about it.

There are indeed a number of different aspects to be grasped. Besides the relationship with the Passion and death of Jesus, introducing the idea of the sacrifice of the New Covenant, there is also the idea of food, wonderfully expressed by Jesus himself in his discourse on the bread of life (see John 6. 26–59). Then again there is that aspect of the Eucharist as being given to the Church, as principle and expression of the Church's unity.

All these aspects were affirmed by Christ himself, as also by Saint Paul. But these various functions of the Eucharist, as sacrifice, as food and as sacrament of unity, together presuppose that Christ is truly though mysteriously present with his body and with his blood in the consecrated bread and wine. It seems best therefore to begin with this notion of the presence of Christ in the Eucharist, which has given rise in time past as also today, to so many controversies, debates and efforts to explain what this really means.

You remember Christ's words over the bread : *"This is my Body."* They are simple words, words that could not be simpler. There is a subject, a verb of affirmation and a complement.

If we now turn to the discourse on the bread of life recorded by Saint John, we cannot help being struck by the force and realism used by Jesus there too. It is one of his most remarkable discourses.

In it, Christ offers himself to mankind as food, as bread come down from heaven, as the bread given by God himself. At the outset, we understand Christ to be the bread of life because he is the Word of God : he feeds us with his truth and with his teaching. But by an imperceptible transition, Jesus then passes on to the Eucharist. And here his discourse acquires a nearly shocking realism : *"He who eats my flesh and drinks my blood has eternal life."* And he repeats the same statement several times, as though afraid of not being understood – so often indeed that the listening Jews were horrified. To understand their sense of outrage and how at the same time their sense of outrage underlines the objective, realistic character of the Lord's words, we have to put ourselves in those Jews' place as they listened to him talking of eating the flesh of the Son of Man, and above all of drinking his blood.

For, be it not forgotten, according to Jewish law, blood was regarded as the symbol of life and was categorically forbidden as food. Even now, Jews never eat meat that has not previously been drained of blood. The very idea of drinking blood was abhorrent. It was out of the question to drink the life-principle.

For people who had been brought up from childhood to think of drinking blood as something absolutely forbidden and abominable, their reaction on hearing Jesus' words was physical nausea. They were appalled, and we can see why. *"This is intolerable language! How could anyone accept it?"* (John 6. 60). They left Jesus and went away. But, we observe, Jesus did not retract one word of what he had been saying; the Jews had understood him perfectly. All he said to the Apostles was : *"What about you, do you want to go away too?* And then it was that Simon Peter made his famous reply : *" Lord, who shall we go to? You have the message of eternal life."* (John 6. 67).

If we compare this discourse on the Eucharistic Bread with the account of the institution of the Lord's Supper, we realize that Jesus' words : *"This is my Body"* have to be understood in their ordinary, concrete sense : they mean the body of Christ, the blood of Christ.

Furthermore, this is the sense in which Christians interpreted the words in earliest times. (*See* 1 Cor. 10 & 11. *'The bread that we break is a communion with the body of Christ."* (10. 16). *"Anyone who eats the bread or drinks the cup of the Lord unworthily will be behaving unworthily towards the body and blood of the Lord."* (11. 27)). According to Christian faith, Christ's body is really – I do not say physically – present in the bread, and his blood really present in the wine. We have, at once, to believe in this presence and also to believe that this presence is not like other presences. There is no word to express it, since there is no other example of this mode of presence in nature. The mode may be called spiritual, but it is none the less as real as, if not more real than, the presence of a being of flesh and blood. And Christ himself suggests as much, without modifying any of the brutal realism of his discourse, by concluding with these words : *"The spirit is what gives life, the flesh has nothing to offer."* (John 6. 63). And this is the Christian faith, simple and strong.

The moment, of course, that we try to imagine what the Eucharistic presence of Christ actually is, we find ourselves in a maze of explanations which would require a theological training to unravel. And it is only fair to admit that theology has succeeded in making this mode of presence intelligible at least to some degree, or at least in demonstrating what it is not.

It is hard to steer a course between interpretations

F

tending on the one hand to physical realism, and on the other to pure symbolism : both tendencies equally wrong. Physical realism as an interpretation springs naturally enough from any imaginitive or tangible representation of the mystery, and this is particularly difficult to avoid, given the way human beings understand things, and is indeed perfectly legitimate, provided always that we merely regard it as a way of representing the reality of the presence, while knowing all the while that the presence is of a totally different order. Christ is in no sense "shut up" in the host or in the tabernacle.

This truly real presence is called sacramental. The mode of presence, as we have already said, is unique : a supernatural and divine presence of Christ's humanity. Thus, it is neither purely symbolic nor purely physical. Jesus is not in the bread or wine as in a place. When we eat the consecrated bread, we do not physically touch the Body of Christ. No one who tried to explain this too precisely will ever succeed in producing a true definition. The Eucharist is still unchanged, for all the explanations, and so will remain until the end of time.

And it all depends on what we mean by presence. When we discuss this we enter the realm of philosophy and find ourselves obliged to use technical terms, as in all forms of science. Thus, philosophically speaking, presence is an analogical concept, by which we mean that there are a number of ways of being present. I am present to you, because I am sitting only a few feet away from you. We are talking – that constitutes another way of being present to one another. You may pick up the telephone and speak to a friend : again, you are present to him, despite the physical distance, in yet another way.

So the modes of presence are very varied. When we say that Christ is really present in the Eucharist, we mean to convey that a link of presence has been set up between the bread and the wine on the one hand, and the Body and Blood of Christ on the other.

Christ is now living in the glory of the Father – a non-terrestrial life – and hence his presence can never take a terrestrial form. Each and every one of the hosts consecrated throughout the world is related to the presence of Christ, without Christ's being either changed or multiplied. That magnificent Latin hymn *Adoro te devote* admirably states the orthodox faith : it says that neither sight, nor taste, nor touch can detect the presence of Christ; but only, among five senses, hearing leads us into the heart of the mystery, by allowing us to hear Christ's words : *This is my Body*, and so to adhere to them by faith : and this faith makes it possible for us to share Christ's own understanding of the mystery that he himself has instituted.

Thus in a world far beyond the senses is where we have to site the Eucharist and take our part in it, not that the Lord may not occasionally grant us feelings of joy, of fulfilment, of certitude, known as sensible graces.

And now, to speak of the Eucharist as sacrifice – since this above all was the reason why Christ instituted the Eucharist. We affirm that by this presence and by the consecration at Mass, we are brought into relationship with the sacrifice on the Cross. This is an aspect of the Eucharistic sacrifice which is frequently under-emphasized, although the very words of consecration declare it by using the words of the Lord himself : *"Do this in memory of me."* And the Apostle Paul is even more explicit : *"Until the Lord comes, therefore, every time you eat this bread and drink this cup, you are proclaiming his death."* (1 Cor. 11. 26)

We proclaim his passion; and by communion we are united to the sacrifice of Christ and share in its fruits.

I have already mentioned that the Christian life consists in reliving the mystery of Christ. By the same token, we have also to relive his passion and his death on the Cross, and this is what gives a hidden and almost infinite dimension to our sufferings, to our troubles, as well as the quality of participating, in the name of mankind, in all suffering.

One of the fruits of communion in the Eucharistic sacrifice should be precisely this : to help us to live this particular truth.

The Eucharistic sacrifice is also the pre-eminent sacrifice of praise. For Christ's offering of himself is now consummated in the eternal glory of the Resurrected Lord eternally praising his Father, and of this praise the offering of the Eucharistic sacrifice is the highest form. We too have our part in this praise.

I need not perhaps insist on the aspect of the Eucharist as communion. In this sacrament, we communicate truly with the Body and Blood of Christ as with the food of life, and this is bestowed on us when we take our part in the sacrifice from which this food derives its life-giving power.

Since Christ is forever interceding with the Father, Christ's prayer is also truly present with him in the Sacrament. This permanence of Christ at prayer in the Eucharist we recognize and show forth by the continual reservation of the Sacrament in church or in Christian communities, as a constant invitation for us to unite ourselves at all times to the Lord's own adoration and intercession.

Here we are of course talking of a free, more personal, more intimate act of devotion to the Eucharist, but one which should be seen as perfectly consistent with our faith in and love for the person of the Lord. I say this, since the reservation and veneration of the Sacrament of the Altar in extension of the Mass are often misunderstood and sometimes even deliberately suppressed on the grounds of somehow infringing the completeness of the Sacrifice, or of being contrary to the wishes of Christ, its author.

It is however perfectly consistent with faith in Christ and with the love we bear him, that, believing in his presence in the Eucharist, we should wish to adore that presence, using the outward sign to strengthen our faith and to focus our prayer. Today we tend to forget that it is our nature to need visible things to raise us towards the invisible. And this is all the more true where the Eucharist is concerned since the Eucharist is both sign and reality at once. The presence and cult of the Holy Sacrament help us to enter into Christ's prayer and permanently associate ourselves with it.

There are of course Christians and liturgiologists who think otherwise. And we ought to have great respect for freedom in the Church of God, especially over the various, genuine ways in which people express their faith and prayer. Tolerance and respect for the legitimate opinions of others are Christian virtues. And the first place to practise them is among ourselves! I am always shocked to see how easily, in Christian communities, factions arise over opinions or ways of doing things, which are not obligatory, and are therefore a matter of free choice. People prompted by their love for Christ and by the logic of their faith to express themselves towards the Holy Sacrament by adoration or by exterior veneration should feel free to do so.

I wish the intimate, extra-liturgical devotion to the Eucharist to be respected and admitted among you. And now, be sure of it, in a secularized world, characterized by materialism and ceaseless activity, people have more than ever a need to hold on to signs of the invisible. The Eucharist, more than any other, reminds them of the presence of Christ in their midst. This is good in itself. Consider your own experience, ask other people too, and you will discover how great a part adoration of the Holy Sacrament has played in maintaining, in nourishing and in developing your life of prayer. Should we be wrong in thinking – when we look at the progress of the Eucharist through the centuries – that this role of the Eucharistic Presence in comforting the faithful and sustaining their prayer was intended by Christ when he instituted the sacrament?

We ought to regard the Eucharist as an inestimable treasure. How amazing it is, once you start thinking about it! The Church could have got rid of the Eucharist centuries ago! Considering all the heresies, all the attacks, all the minimizing interpretations of which the Eucharist has been the object : it would have sufficed to cease celebrating it, or to cease consecrating priests, and that would have been the end of it. Yet Christians of all traditions despite the strife, despite the clash of doctrine have always retained the Eucharistic celebration. People may argue about it, but it is always there, an irrefutable and abiding sign of the Son of Man's incomprehensible love for his fellow men.

VI

The New Demands of the Lord's Commandment

"Who is my neighbour?"

We now come to the problem lying at the heart of human life, at the heart of Christianity and therefore, be it said, at the heart of the message of our Fraternity, the badge of which – chosen by Brother Charles of Jesus – is a heart surmounted by a cross.

Love is both cause and law of human activity. We could even say that where there is no love, there is no action and there is no life. Love, however, is very complicated and mysterious. By love and in love, man rises above himself to reach a foretaste of eternity. Man fulfils himself by love, when he loves but, above all perhaps, when he is loved. Man cannot be entirely himself without being loved or without trying to love.

The most cursory glance at human nature and at the world today will show us how strong and dynamic love can be, and how complex too the problems that it causes. And note, that all the feelings and contradictory conditions that it produces are designated by this one word, love.

There is passionate love: blind, violent, instinctive, paralysing the intellect and driving man to actions which on occasion can culminate in self-destruction. Mark too the burden of many modern songs: sadness, disappointment, love affairs that have gone wrong; here you have a kind of

love that can lead to suicide pacts and the ultimate nega-
tion of hope.

Then there is instinctive love, also very powerful : maternal love, paternal love. I use the word instinctive in its
truest sense – of a love that springs from the depths of
nature. Love like this is capable of highest heroism. So we
see very ordinary people, once they have become fathers,
capable of acts of extra-ordinary unselfishness.

But instinctive love, however exalted, can develop flaws,
and distortions. Mother-love can be vitiated by unconscious
egoism, producing great suffering and even profound dis-
turbance in the children.

The thing that usually disfigures love is the lack of clear-
sightedness or intelligence. It is not easy to know how to
love – properly.

Then there is loving devotion – a condition in which all
our activities can become subordinated, not necessarily to
the greater good of the person who we sincerely wish to
serve and believe that we are serving.

And finally there is what we might call ideological love.
This is the love characteristic of certain types of intellectual.
When Marx was analysing the conditions of the London
working-classes and writing the first draft of *Das Kapital*
in his lowly bed-sittingroom, he was sincerely affected by
love for the oppressed – and this embodied itself in an
ideology. Marx worked out a new way of life, which he supposed would liberate people from all the material and
moral evils observed by him at the outset of the industrial
era.

At his level, owing to abstractions and ideals imposed on
people for their own good, love is unintentionally the cause
of violence, oppression and suffering – the effects of the
built-in errors of an ideological system regarded as final and
exclusively correct.

It is not easy therefore to love in the right way. In con-
jugal love, in maternal love, as well as in friendship and
devotion to our brothers, there must be enlightenment or

there will be no true notion of what the real good of the beloved is.

Love should be man's most perfect and most selfless act. And it cannot be that, unless it is enlightened and guided by truth. Love cannot be love without truth. Without truth, there is no certain way of escaping the inevitable pitfalls of egoism concealed in passionate love or in instinctive love. True love is never selfish, as passionate or instinctive love nearly always is – to some degree at least – for in these there is always a tendency to make the need to be loved in return take precedence over a true giving of oneself to the beloved. Loving consists in desiring the good of the beloved above all else, and in seeking that good at the cost of self-sacrifice. Perfect love demands that the will be free and the intellect clear and receptive to truth.

Let us now consider the Lord's commandment. God teaches us that there is a close bond between loving God and loving our brothers. Jesus, when questioned about this, replied : *"You must love the Lord your God with all your heart, with all your soul, and with all your mind. This is the greatest and the first commandment. The second resembles it: You must love your neighbour as yourself. On these two commandments hang the whole Law, and the Prophets too."* (Matt. 22. 37).

This commandment is supplemented by one that Jesus himself gave to his disciples : *"I give you a new commandment: Love one another. Just as I have loved you, you too must love one another."* (John 13. 34).

The fact that these two loves are so closely linked means that no one can love God without loving his brother. As Saint John says : *"Anyone who says, 'I love God', and hates his brother, is a liar; a man who does not love the brother that he can see cannot love God whom he has never seen. So this is the commandment that he has given us: that anyone who loves God must also love his brother."* (1 John 20–21).

But the converse must also be stated : that no one can

love his brother perfectly, unless he loves God. And when we speak of loving perfectly, it may be that he loves God, although he as yet does not know him. A man cannot love his brothers perfectly without having already escaped from self, without having already discovered an absolute; and when this absolute is God, or Christ, clearly known and truly believed in, then most light is bestowed to enlighten and guide that love.

Some too are travelling towards a God as yet unknown but already present to their love through some ideal unselfishly pursued. We are indeed all travelling, since we can never achieve a truly perfect love : perfect love being the goal which we are trying to reach. Hence people who do not know God because they have never had the opportunity of knowing him, can nonetheless be already travelling in the right direction; these can indeed learn truly how to love.

We shall be judged by how we have loved. Or more precisely, love will be our judge; for God is love, and Love will judge us, and must be able to recognize us for his.

And here we think of the dramatic parable, in which Christ shows us how he will recognize those who are his on Judgement Day : *"I was hungry and you gave me food; I was thirsty and you gave me drink; I was a stranger and you made me welcome; naked and you clothed me; sick and you visited me; in prison and you came to see me. Then the virtuous will reply: 'Lord, when did we see you hungry and feed you; or thirsty and give you drink? When did we see you a stranger and make you welcome; naked and clothe you; sick or in prison and go to see you?' And the King will answer: 'I tell you solemnly, in so far as you did this to one of the least of these brothers of mine, you did it to me'"* (Matt. 25. 35–40).

Here we have both the affirmation of the bond of love existing between God and man, and the assurance that people will be recognized by the Lord as belonging to him, even though they have not recognized him on earth : their hearts having met him without knowing.

Christ has given us a new commandment, and he himself calls it his commandment. What is new about this commandment? For, from what we have just been saying it appears that the link between the first two commandments was already known and lived before the Incarnation. It is this : Christ, by affirming that this commandment, teaches us that there is an essential link between it and him. *"Just as I have loved you, you too must love one another."* So ever since Christ was born into this world there has been something new about love.

And this new factor consists precisely in that God became incarnate, and that in consequence man has been raised, transfigured in a dimension that he could never have conceived. When talking of love, we have to remember that no one can love who has not himself first been loved. And Christ, most especially by his agony on the Cross, reveals the compassionate love with which God loves us. He has revealed a love, at once immense, infinite, full of tenderness and compassion, reaching each of us individually through the wounded heart of Christ who dies for us. This is the revelation of God as Love, and of a compassionate love drawing near to men, rejecting no one however sinful, since it is his nature to save the fallen, to heal the sick and to strengthen the feeble. In Christ human personality is invested with a new dignity, since man has become the son of God; whether he actually achieves this sonship through the grace of baptism into the Church, or whether he is called to achieve it, such henceforth is his destiny. Man can no longer be loved as he used to be loved; henceforth he has to be loved with the strength and respect due to God, simply because he is man. It is a very great but extremely rare thing, to be able to love a man sincerely, simply because he is a man.

When we love people, we love them because of the qualities which we admire in them, or for reasons of gratitude, or perhaps because they have something to offer us, or because we have received something from them, or because we are attracted to them. But to love a man simply because he is a man, is very hard. And people hardly ever do it. Let us take an illustration from the youth of Saint Francis of Assisi. When Francis, overcoming his repugnance, kissed an appalling-looking leper as his brother, that day he loved the man because he was a man and hence the image and presence of Christ. By tenderly kissing the wretch, Francis was kissing Jesus in person.

This is what gives the commandment of love its universality. Man, whatever his race, culture, qualities, even the man we hate, who inspires us with nothing but hostility, with whom we have nothing in common, and who does not even speak the same language : this man by virtue of being man deserves our love, and bears within him an element of the infinite.

Another new factor is that, since the Incarnation of the Word and the Redemption operated by him, man is better fitted to know what is his own greatest good, and that he is a co-heir with Christ, as Saint Paul says. And by virtue of this, he has the possibility here-below of possessing infinite riches, the riches of faith; not only that, but divine adoption, explicit knowledge of Christ, real and intimate union with him, and finally the hope of everlasting life – all this has been available to man, since Christ came on earth. We know about his wealth, and every man has the right to possess it here on earth. And we have a duty to respect this heritage left to us, by Christ as something destined for all men.

And finally what is new and what Christ particularly values is the indefinite demand implicit in the commandment of love. I say indefinite advisedly; I cannot call it infinite, our potentialities and our lives having a term.

Although Christ said "*Love one another as I have loved you*", it is nonetheless a fact that no one could ever claim to love his brothers as much as Jesus has loved them. All the

same, this is what we are obliged to try to do : the commandment of love is therefore the only commandment
that can never be fulfilled. The other commandments
involve definite actions which can be carried out to the
letter; as for instance, to tell the truth, to respect the
property of others, not to commit adultery. But we never
succeed in discharging the obligations of the commandment of love, since we can never love enough. The commandment entails an indefinite demand : we have not got
the right to stop growing in love. It is a sin against love to
refuse to grow in charity. We disobey Christ's commandment when we halt; only he who ceaselessly advances
towards love obeys the commandment.

How are we to obey Christ's commandment? How are
we to love properly? How are we to love, beyond the
passions, beyond errors, beyond our own limitations? What
must we do to love our brothers perfectly? And here we
have the problem of the relationship between love and the
spontaneous, sometimes passionate, emotions, our sym-
pathies and antipathies. We are as it were caught in a net.
Moreover, love must not be blind, since it is only able to
grow in the light of truth. These are two questions that are
certainly worth reflection.

If we want to grow in love and learn to love perfectly,
we must continually be in search of the truth and of people's
true good. I say search, since the true good of our brothers,
their greatest good, is not an abstraction but something concrete, variable according to circumstance. There are in fact
two kinds of good for man.

There is the eternal and absolute good, which is his salvation. And this is something that he can already possess to
some degree on earth by hope. No one has the right to take
this away from anyone else. The search for this absolute
good for others is the purpose of the apostolate and mission of the Church.

But there is another good, call it the greater good, which
is not absolute, but the best possible, immediate, concrete,

at once temporal and spiritual : and man has a right to this too. And this is not easy to define, being variable and relative. It varies according to circumstance, from person to person, from family to family. It is conditioned by the greater good of a nation, of a human type, of an environment, and even of a political regime. It is an immediate, temporal good : and we have a duty to pursue it.

So then it is a general rule that we cannot try to achieve the perfection of love without seeking sincerely by every effort to discover what the greater good would be for those whom we love.

Loving needs an apprenticeship : we should be wrong to think that we have a natural gift for it. And in this very apprenticeship resides the hard vocation of the Christian. The truth of this must be evident to anyone familiar with Christ's message. But, take an ordinary human example, the history of a marriage, for instance, from wedding-day to deathbed what a saga, what ups and downs, what an apprenticeship the parties have to serve before they make their marriage good !

And so the first point to be made is that we cannot learn how to love unless we first resolve to renounce ourselves. Conscious or unconscious selfishness is one of the major obstacles to loving.

The Lord has warned us about this : *"If anyone wants to be a follower of mine, let him renounce himself"* (Matt. 16. 24). We must be free to love; and the first liberation consists in freeing ourselves from self. Too often we are imprisoned in ourselves, we are slaves to so many things, we are limited. And because of this, what suffering we cause !

Renunciation of self consists initially in mastering our passions. This is self-evident. I have already mentioned the instinctive feelings of like and dislike that enslave us. All love worthy of the name is beyond the reach of passion.

Another important aspect of liberation from self lies in being detached from our own opinions. This particular

form of freedom is essential if we are to remain open to
progress, to mutual enrichment of mind, and of course is
also the essential prerequisite in our search for truth. We
ought to be detached from our own opinions in so far as
they are ours, since we ought always to be objective in our
judgements and faithful to truth. We must also be open
and receptive to the views of other people. There is, after
all, no *a priori* reason why our own ideas should be intrin-
sically right and those of others mistaken or merely second-
best to ours. Dissension and bitterness spring up when we
think we know better than our neighbour. The practice of
detachment opens the way to truth.

Now consider the relationship between love and the
moral law.

Today we have a better grasp – a sign of our progress –
of how the commandment of love is both basis and summary of the moral law, although the true nature and
demands of love cannot be defined without reference to
the moral law.

Genuine love can only exist in the light of the truth that
regulates the actions of men. Take for instance adultery or
divorce. People will justify the break-up of the home, however disastrous its effects for the children, on the grounds
of loyalty to passionate love. People manufacture their own
sincerity, and their own law. But the moral obligation is
still there, the purpose of which is to safeguard the
demands of proper love. Love is of course the only law,
but not any kind of love. The essential quality of love must
be preserved despite our mistakes, our self-centred opinions,
our emotions : and the preservation of this is what the
obligations of the moral law are for. Left to ourselves, we
are not always equipped to be faithful to the demands of
proper love, and there are two reasons why this is so : first
because of our own limitations, mistakes and emotions; and
secondly because the ultimate goal of love eludes us, just
as God's demands for our perfection and our destiny as
sons of God pass our ability to understand. It will not do

to minimize the demands of the Christian vocation. Love at its most perfect entails an absolute respect for oneself and for the person whom one loves, in the light of eternity.

And this is therefore the place to explain a text in the Gospel about how we should love our neighbour. The words are often misunderstood and may even shock the over-idealistic : *"You must love your neighbour as yourself"* (Matt. 19. 19; 22. 39). What a very mediocre ideal, some people may think. Shouldn't I love my neighbour more than I love myself, Shouldn't I love him at the expense of myself? Yes, of course you should. But that is not what this commandment means. This one is the foundation of all morality. It is deeply concerned with the dignity of man – the basis of all Christian morality. And its meaning is that you cannot respect human dignity in other people unless you first respect it in yourself.

So here, loving yourself is used in the sense that Jesus himself defined when he commanded us to love one another as he has loved us; we have therefore an obligation to love ourselves. Each of us is obliged to love himself as Christ loves him; in other words, I am not free to do what I like with myself, since the law of love is binding on me too. I am loved by Christ, I do not belong to myself. What Christ wants of me is that I should conform to his Gospel and that I should love my brothers as he himself has loved them. What then I should want for myself is that the law of Christ should be made perfect in me. Christ loves me, as he loves other men, my brothers. Hence no one can dispose of his own person merely as he himself pleases, without putting himself outside that love that Christ bears for him. We must be aware of being loved by Christ, and keep reminding ourselves that because of this love we do not have the right to dispose of ourselves as we please. We do not belong to ourselves, but to Christ who has redeemed us and who loved us first.

Renouncing ourselves and loving ourselves as Christ loves us prepares us for that highest form of love that

flows from the heart of Christ : and this love is governed
by the code of the beatitudes. You have only to read the
Sermon on the Mount (Matt. 5. 3) to realize how difficult
or perhaps even impossible it is to define the beatitudes in
rational terms. What mysterious realities Christ must contemplate, for him to proclaim as blessed the poor, those
who weep, those who thirst for righteousness, the compassionate, those who work for peace and those who are per-
secuted in the cause of righteousness, those who bear insult
for the sake of Christ. The Kingdom of God is theirs; they
will be consoled, be satisfied, be sons of God and will see
God. Even more, right now they are *to rejoice and be
glad.*

The beatitudes form a living whole; you cannot separate
them from each other. You cannot take poverty from
gentleness, nor from peace, nor from compassion. For
indeed what would be the good of poverty without peace,
gentleness and humility? The beatitudes are a code of love.
we cannot love as Christ loves without poverty, and we
must understand that the beatitudes express and help to
achieve that liberation from self without which we are in
no state to love others as God wishes us to love them.

The absence of poverty, the love of money, the thirst for
power and for self-importance are among the most immediate and abiding causes of injustice, of lack of love and
respect for other people. We cannot love our brothers
unless we learn to put ourselves in their place; we cannot
love them if we consider ourselves to be better and worthier
than they are. Love will only come to full flowering in the
hearts of humble people of good-will. This does not of
course prevent us from seeing other people as they are, and
they are all different enough in all conscience : some are
reasonably educated, others not, and some are better than
others. But where human personality and the basic good
that is in everyone, and dignity and conscience are concerned, we have no right either to judge or to scorn anyone,
or to suppose ourselves in any way superior.

G

Humility manifests itself in availability and willingness to serve. As an attitude of soul, as a virtue, humility is in small regard today, yet indispensable to love. That peace of heart which is one of its fruits, that peace which Christ gives us, warning us that he does not give it "as the world gives it" : that is the condition on which depends that other external peace which men desire. No institution can procure and maintain peace, if men themselves have not themselves become peaceful by learning to liberate themselves from their own self-centredness.

Without compassion and forgiveness, our love will not be like the love that moved the heart of Christ. We should do well to recall one of the Lord's stern warnings : *"Do not judge, and you will not be judged; for the judgements you give are the judgements you will get."*

Without respect for others, there is no brotherly love. Not to judge is not to condemn. We have to understand our neighbour as he understands himself and judges himself. Once again, this does not mean that we are not to be realistic. But it is one thing to judge behaviour, an action, an attitude of mind, and a very different one to judge a person.

And here is something else that respect for our brothers requires of us : that we do not speak ill of them, even when what we say is true. We do not have the right to ruin a man's reputation : a good reputation is something to which everyone has a right. We have only to put ourselves in his place and ask how we should feel if we were being traduced behind our back, to see how serious such behaviour is. Saint James has much to say about the harm that a wagging tongue can do : *"Nobody must imagine that he is religious while he still goes on deceiving himself and not keeping control over his tongue; anyone who does this has the wrong idea of religion"* (James 1. 26). *"Among all the parts of the body, the tongue is a whole wicked world in itself; it infects the whole body"* (James 3. 2–12).

What misery, what tragedies, what broken homes, what

despair – caused by the ill-considered language of people unaware of the harm that they were doing.

Next I would remind you of the respect that we most particularly owe to those whom Christ calls "little ones". By this, the Lord means children, and also men who are not sufficiently educated to master or judge things and hence find themselves at the mercy of others. They are vulnerable and we can easily harm them. *"Anyone who is an obstacle to bring down one of these little ones who have faith in me would be better drowned in the depths of the sea with a great millstone round his neck"* (Matt. 18. 6). Christ's anger echoes through these words. Respect for men, particularly for the weakest, is important to God – and how very rare it is!

Lastly, on this same topic, the revelation of love opens the way to true friendship. Friendship is reciprocal love enriching either party, each being able to enjoy the possessions of the other. Friendship is sharing and communion. It requires that we have learnt to give, but even more that we have learnt how to receive. It is often more difficult to receive, to let ourselves be loved, to accept, than to give. Friendship demands that we let ourselves be loved, that we accept the intrusion of other people into our lives. Friendship pre-supposes that someone should esteem us : we have to receive something from our friend. Whereas in our own feelings which prompt us to give, there is often an element of wanting to fulfil ourselves, whether consciously or unconsciously, by making the gift. People can be very tiresome in the way they show their friendship. Initially, love undeniably requires an apprenticeship. The poets used to say there was an art of love : how right they were!

And now we must consider the meaning of commitment. The individual, according to his state in life and means of action, has a duty to work for the greater good of others. This greater good is something concrete, being both material and spiritual. And here we are not talking of the absolute, eternal good, which is the object of the Church's mission, nor of the apostolic duty devolving on every Christian as such.

The temporal good, the common good of human society is everyone's responsibility, and a Christian has a duty to labour for it by virtue of being a man, a citizen of the world and the member of a city. Naturally, the fact that man is called to an eternal good affects our own view of the greater good of earthly society. Specifically it affects the relationship between the form of society adopted and the right to freedom of religion. Social institutions can be favourable or unfavourable to the right development of human morality. All this must be taken into account, since man does not have two separate goods, or two destinies. You may ask whether a Christian should not be like everyone else and behave like everyone else. A Christian is certainly human like everyone else : in his profession he is a professional man, in his city he is a citizen, in the world a citizen of the world. But the meaning he attaches to life and the concept he has of human nature are different from those of non-Christians. Every concept of human society, unless it be a purely pragmatic one – that is to say, exclusively concerned with organizing the economy and allowing that to dictate what form society shall take – rests on an ideology, and depends on the idea held of the purpose of human life and of what society ought to be and do. Ideology may be defined as a coherent system of thought aiming to give a world-wide interpretation of human problems with a view to establishing a society appropriate to them. Every ideology therefore has as its basis a particular view of man.

As regards the building of the earthly city and in all the activities contributing to it, whether political, economic, scientific or cultural, a Christian in his capacity of citizen will find himself on the side of all who have a respect for freedom and human personality and for the moral and spiritual requirements guaranteeing the dignity of man Certain values a Christian can never forego, society must respect those. At the level of the city and of the normal requirements of decency, Christians fortunately have no monopoly of high-mindedness.

In committing ourselves to the temporal good, we should listen to what the Church has to say in specific cases, but on the whole the choice is ours and the responsibilities are ours too. But there are the moral values to which a Christian must remain true when committing himself to temporal activities of this sort :

The first question that a Christian should ask himself is this : what today are we to understand by "neighbour"? Who is our neighbour? For, if we are convinced of the duty that we have to translate our love for others into action and concrete commitment, we are also aware that our field of operation must necessarily be limited. We ourselves are limited, and our limits when we confront the almost limitless needs of others will make us seem sadly impotent; many of us may feel too discouraged to go on. We do however realize that the demands of the Lord's commandment are not so much fulfilled by the quantity of our activities as by the quality of the love that inspires them. This notwithstanding, and given conditions in the world today, translation of love into action must be governed by a proper notion of who our neighbour is and of the duties incumbent on ourselves once we have discovered his identity.

Who is our neighbour? As the original meaning of the word implies, it means that we are bound to exercise charity in ways co-ordinate to the nearness of the recipient. But the world as it is today has virtually abolished the old meaning of nearness. In olden days, a neighbour was someone who lived near you : geography was the determining factor. There were no rapid means of communication, contacts were regional at their widest; towns and villages were autonomous communities. The neighbour was first our family, then the people living next-door, and finally the other people in the village.

But today we cannot define our neighbour in these terms.

It is much more complicated now : human relations are now world-wide; towns, regions, nations and continents are interdependent, economically speaking if not otherwise as well.

In defining the neighbour anew, probably the best thing to say would be that anyone who is justified in expecting something from us is our neighbour; and this means that for love of Christ we ought to give him what he expects from us. Thus, suppose there are a number of poor families living in a shanty-town in sub-human conditions on the edge of my city : what are they justified in expecting from me? They are justified in expecting me, as a citizen of that city, to do everything in my power to urge the municipal council to solve the housing problem. This of course, does not absolve me from trying to put such a wretched and unjust situation right as quickly as possible by my own efforts and those of my community. If, in olden times, my own efforts might have sufficed to achieve what the law of love requires of me, today this is not the case. We have to act, not at individual but at city level. To do this, we must get together, take counsel together. This is our political duty – and possibly then decide to bring pressure to bear on the authorities by informing and activating public opinion by means of a campaign in the press. Such are the present dimensions of the second commandment.

Similiarly as regards our responsibilities in wartime or in times of preparation for war. The hundreds of thousands of human beings experiencing the horrors of war expect something from the rest of the world. We can no longer say that these people's conditions do not impose any duty of action on us, by virtue of their being far away and of our not being directly responsible or involved, happily being citizens of another country : no, these too are our neighbour.

So the next thing to decide is what we can and should do. Here, we find ourselves obliged to act through inter-national organizations, be they official or private; and the whole question of the relationship between rich countries and poor countries opens up before us. The solutions to problems like these will certainly have to be political ones. And so we find ourselves developing a sense of international political responsibility. If we mean to carry out the command to love our neighbour to the uttermost, we inevitably find ourselves committed to political activities. But these are difficult, complicated and normally produce only long-term results. Again we are tempted to feel discouraged and selfishly to confine ourselves to solving specific problems involving the well-being of our own region or of our own family.

The majority of changes achieved in the world are prepared long in advance, and therefore need clear-sightedness, much hard work, and great selflessness and perseverance on the part of those dedicated to achieving them.

Such at any rate are a few thoughts on the demands that loving our neighbour will make on us. Like you, I am still asking the question that the scribe put to Jesus : "Who then is my neighbour?'

This broadening of the concept of our neighbour must not make us forget the priority of our duties. People who have professional or family duties should discharge these fully. There would be something very wrong, and indeed unnatural, if parents were to neglect the up-bringing of their own children, on the grounds of having to devote their time and energy to some commitment of wider scope. But there would be something equally wrong in shutting oneself up in family matters to the exclusion of all extraneous duties.

From all of which it follows that it is hard, if not impossible, in the great majority of cases, to decide what people's greater good may be and to do something towards achieving it, unless we collectively take serious thought and action, whether it be through some institution, organization or political party. Individual acts of charity have not exactly had their day since there are unlimited opportunities for these, but in themselves they no longer suffice.

And here I am talking of the way we should practise Christian charity – something very personal prompted by the warmth and perceptiveness imparted by the Spirit of Christ to those who follow him; for this duty, though not easy, even so cannot be said to raise any great problem. What I mean here is a new duty, the scope of which is much more difficult to appreciate. For example : compare the position of Saint Louis, King of France, with that of the President of the United States, the chief executive of a great modern state. Saint Louis had a simple social situation to deal with, where all he needed, for governing well, was a sense of justice, or virtue and of responsibility for the well-being of his people. The private Christian virtues of the sovereign directly affected the government and indeed conditioned its particular political flavour. In the case of the President of the United States, we are confronted with the most enormous and complex democracy imaginable. To govern a country so vast and so intensively industrialized, the President has to collaborate with cohorts of specialists and experts of every kind : commissions, subcommissions, committees of experts, statistics, opinion-polls, computers, electronic brains. And all these have to be set to work before the President of the USA can decide and effect his economic or political programmes.

With an apparatus of government as complicated as this, it is much more difficult to preserve a human face of love and justice to go with it. There is a real risk that government will become completely depersonalized. Yet we cannot possibly do without this sort of team-work, as much for planning our projects as for bringing them to good effect. And more and more people will have to be taught a greater and greater sense of responsibility towards one another; under-privileged countries, for instance, cannot hope to escape from their poverty unless they assume responsibility for themselves and learn to organize their own affairs.

The best will in the world and all the love that goes with

it are no longer enough to give a human face to the lives of people living in some countries. Take the appalling conditions in north-east Brazil. To improve conditions there, it would first take teams of economists working for months and probably years to decide what ought to be done to improve the agricultural yield, internal trade, means of communication and industrial development. Because of the climate and soil-conditions, part of the population may well have to be re-settled elsewhere. Such is the scope of the problems and obstacles that commonsense, technology and desire for social justice have to overcome before any tangible results can be obtained. And although human institutions are often the negligent cause of these problems, they are not always in a position to put them right again : it takes time and resources; and governmental activity has its limitations. But the more human activity has to be channelled through intermediaries, through institutions and organizations, the greater the risk of its losing its human face – the face of justice and love. And this particular difficulty can be encounted almost anywhere. In a factory employing ten or fifteen thousand work-people, is it or is it not reasonable to think that truly human relations can be established between management and workers? Can a special human-relations service solve this problem, or not? Suppose the human-relations service were to adopt psychological techniques : would this be good or bad?

The Christian must try to fulfil the demands of justice and love within the institutions where he works : in professional groups, trade unions, political parties, town councils, local organizations, any organization.

One of the most urgent and serious problems now facing mankind is to discover a way of making economic development serve the true development of human personality. To work at this is a duty of Christian charity.

In whichever way a Christian decides to commit himself, there are certain values that he has a duty to safeguard for the sake of human dignity and human rights.

In the increasing complexity of our problems and the solutions that we propose for them, it is most important that people should preserve their freedom of judgement. The enslavement of the mind is not an illusory danger. People talk a lot about the liberation of man : but in trying to achieve this at top speed, there is a risk of becoming enslaved to systems, to slogans and to over-simplified solutions. There is always the danger of becoming no more than the passive tool of a party. Thinking for oneself, and a sense of personal responsibility, are often represented as obstacles to efficient large-scale action.

My job is to warn you of the danger; not to offer you the solution. Remember that, for a follower of Christ, man is more precious and more important than anything else in the universe, more important than the political order, more important than any economic or ideological system, be it what it may.

As well as intellectual freedom, we must also preserve our objectivity, especially when we find ourselves having to decide what the true good of men actually is in a given situation. Man was created to be happy. We must feel for his happiness and be prepared to ask ourselves in what his happiness resides. It may be hard, but it has to be done. And this is where we have to consider the relationship between the temporal order and the eternal good. Consider the situation of men in a totalitarian society, whether socialist or not, who are deprived of freedom of expression. Religious liberty is part and parcel of intellectual freedom, and one manifestation of it.

What part does the Church have to play in all this?

In the course of human development throughout the last two thousand years, the Church has hitherto played an important part in the evolution of society and culture. The role of the Church has been very clearly defined by the Second Vatican Council : as Christ himself solemnly declared, his Kingdom is not of this world. The establishing of the Kingdom of God takes place in the individual conscience. Often, therefore, the Kingdom is among us without our realizing it; its frontiers are invisible. The Church is a society, and hence has an institutional structure, but this latter is determined by the spiritual goal and mission of the Church, and is never directly a part of the temporal order.

To state the matter clearly : the freedom and salvation brought by Christ are essentially liberation from sin and moral evil. Indirectly, therefore, by the growth of love, the fruit of liberation from sin, the work of the Church contributes to the liberation of people from all forms of oppression and injustice to which temporal institutions fall a prey. This must be clearly understood. The Church's only means of reaching men is by love; the free constraint of love is the only constraint that the Church can exercise over people.

Christianity is not an ideology : and one cannot say this too often. Christianity is not a system or a recipe for the running of temporal affairs. Hence, Christianity and Marxism cannot be represented as rival systems. They do not exist on the same plane. Marxism is a political ideology, and Christianity is not. Certainly however they are opposed : and if you say that marxist atheism is opposed to the profession of Christian faith and to a spiritual view of the world, then naturally I agree, since here we are talking of things on the same plane. But you cannot oppose Christianity to communism in practical politics, since the former does not embody itself in any particular form of government or society. To communism, on the other hand, you can perfectly well oppose various other brands of socialism.

Similiarly, the evangelization of the poor, the establishing of more equitable relations between men, the coming of the reign of love in men's hearts, these are also reflected in institutions. Christ and his Church set men free by transforming the conscience of the individual. But it also happens that the Church, when she deems it opportune, encourages Christians to put their charity into practical form and points out where and how they should instil more justice into earthly society. Hence these great encyclicals of Leo XIII and John XXIII. Those of Leo XIII laid down the broad lines of the social teaching of the Church. Naturally enough, some aspects do not seem applicable to forms of society that have since come into being. Hence the need to distinguish in these doctrines between general principles permanently valid, and their practical application to a given type of society, which is necessarily relative. The early encyclicals of Leo XIII for instance contained practical applications for the industrial and capitalist society of his day, and it is a pity that they were not more widely applied at the time.

Today, however, as our political, economic and sociological conditions grow more and more complicated and require more and more expert knowledge to cope with them, the Church tends to confine herself to reaffirming the broad principles, while leaving their application to competent members of the laity. Nonetheless, the Church keeps her right of judging the moral worth of all human activities, even political ones. In this sense, she is the judge of temporal institutions. But it is not for her, as the Church, to impose them.

For there used to be a time when the Church did determine the political structure of the city : that is to say, in the Christian middle ages. For then you had a society in which the Gospel and the Canon Law of the Church were recognized as law by the state. The Christian religion was the state religion. Today, the secularization of the temporal city is an accomplished fact. The Second Vatican Council signalled the ending of that period of history by promulgating the decree of liberty of conscience. This decree is more important than many people suppose in defining the respective missions of the temporal city and of the Church and in regulating the relations that ought to exist between these two types of society.

The Church in our day can no longer be identified with any form of government. And wherever she is still identified with one, she is now doing her best to disengage. Any link between the Church and a particular form of government entails, sooner or later, the enslavement of the Church to it, or at least a limitation of her freedom of expression by it.

And this leads us to another question : the involvement of bishops and priests in politics. It would seem illogical, on the one hand to insist that the Church should play no part in politics, and on the other to insist on the right of Church leaders to commit themselves to political activities. I suppose one might be able to draw a distinction between what they do as private persons and what they do by virtue of their office. But in the case of people invested with a mission by the Church in the name of Christ, is political commitment right? To be chosen by Christ and given a mission by him is not like having an ordinary job; it means commitment of the whole person to following Christ.

But of course the question is not as simple as that. Priests and bishops, by virtue of their commission as pastors, may find themselves virtually forced into taking action over matters of the temporal order – since evangelization, especially evangelization of the poor, must be concerned with the whole man as he is and as he lives. Paul VI has himself emphasized the close connexion between evangelization and development. (Message of Pope Paul, June 5, 1970, for World Missionary Year.)

Let us consider some examples of the bonds that can exist between bishops and priests, and their people. There are situations where the clergy may be led to take the initiative in the temporal order, when charity or justice demand it of them. This happens when the negligence of a government or when conditions of social injustice become so acute that the pastors of the Church find themselves alone to be in a position to take the necessary remedial action.

Here is an example. In a remote part of one of the countries in the Middle East, there are Christian villages where religious faith is deep but culture decidedly primitive, and whose only defence, amid the surrounding Moslem population, is their bishop. He lives very close to his people and has his home among them. A distant and not particularly sympathetic government leaves these villagers without support or redress against the raids of Moslem nomads who periodically come and burn and pillage the villagers' crops. The bishop being the only person in a position to defend these people, on occasion rides forth at their head to repel the raiders. Here you have a concrete necessity. The bishop identifies himself with his flock; he administers justice, composes their quarrels, resolves family disputes. Without him, his people would have short shrift in the courts.

Would you call this a case of interference by the Church, or admit that here she is acting, in the name of charity and justice, on behalf of a temporal power that is either non-existent, incapable or unjust?

Perhaps you will say that this is an exceptional case. But I choose it on purpose, since it demonstrates my point and I have witnessed this myself. But in the modern world, for all its progress, you can find any number of similar, or at least analogous, situations in which the Church has a duty to intervene. Would it not be true of the bishops of north-east Brazil, for instance, where they have taken the initiative in economic projects such as building barrages, so that their flocks do not starve to death? If these bishops had not done it, no one would have done it.

Moreover, if priests and bishops have a duty to take action in cases of crying need, they have an even more specific duty to inculcate their people with a sense of responsibility for themselves and hence a sense of political responsibility. Here again, team-work and a sense of doing things together, can transform a population and restore to the poor a sense of dignity as human beings. This work of justice and love strikes me as very closely allied to the evangelistic work proper to the Church.

Thirty years ago I used to know a young Jesuit in Chile, who was a true man of God, entirely devoted to the poor and the workers. He was the first member of the clergy to do anything for the working-classes. He started an enormous work of education on individual and trade-union lines for a social class hitherto apathetically resigned to its lot. The effects of his work were remarkable. Yet he never dissociated himself from his priesthood. He died at the age of forty-five, of cancer. Chile went into national mourning, particularly the poor and the working-classes. Radio bulletins on the progress of his illness were followed by a grief-stricken nation.

Different situations compel the Church to act in different ways, while remaining fundamentally faithful to her mission. It would not enter the head of a priest in France or England to found a trade-union: it would not be his business, laymen can do it just as well.

By the same token and corresponding to the evolution of society, Christian trade-unionism has also gone through a transformation. In every sphere, things tend to a greater independence vis-à-vis the Church and a greater responsibility assumed by the laity in temporal affairs. Christians should act according to conscience. The Church's job is to form the Christian conscience to enlighten it and to encourage people to assume their responsibilities in the light of the Gospel.

VII

The Apostolic Mission

"So that the world may believe that you have sent me."

We must now consider the apostolate of the Church. We have already discussed the relationship between temporal commitment and the message and saving work of Christ. We shall confine ourselves to the teachings of the Second Vatican Council. Few Councils indeed have been more explicit or more comprehensive in their treatment of the Church's mission, and you could not do better than to read and meditate on the texts that the Council has produced. The bishops of the entire world having spent months together working to produce these remarkable documents, it is surely not for us to file them away after a cursory glance; rather, we Christians should assimilate what they have to say and put them into effect in our daily lives. If we believe in the Church and in the importance of an Ecumenical Council for elucidating the content of faith under inspiration of the Holy Spirit, we should enter whole-heartedly into this period of assimilation, making it possible for the Council to bear fruit. I shall not be saying anything that is not to be found in the conciliar documents but I think it would be profitable for us to reconsider them and their doctrine together as a whole.

The mission of the Church, basically speaking, is to extend the mission of Christ himself, by proclaiming his message and by guiding men into the way of salvation, by its range of apostolic activities. Christ was quite explicit about this mission when he selected his Apostles and enjoined them, before his Ascension, to disperse and preach his message to all peoples. A mission of this sort, with a commitment to communicating, to sharing and to teaching men to love, flows naturally from love and is a work of love.

Imagine for a moment that you are one of the Apostles : you love Christ passionately, everything you have you have received from him, you are aware of having received an immense universal gift, destined for all mankind. Wouldn't your ruling pre-occupation henceforth be to devote your life to passing on to others what you yourself had so fully and so freely received? So the Church's mission is not solely based on Christ's wish when he instituted a society and endowed it with appropriate means. The Church's mission also flows from a spontaneous demand of charity diffused throughout the whole body of Christ. Love urges Christians on; they cannot be indifferent as regards handing Christ's message on to men, without relying on the divine love dwelling within them. It is the very nature of love to try and spread : this spreading and the practical activities entailed make up the apostolate.

So we can say that every activity contributing to the extension of the Kingdom of God belongs to the apostolate. This is a very broad conception, in the sense that we are not merely speaking now of the setting up of the Church as such, but of any extension of the Kingdom of God; for all men, whoever they are and whatever their religion and situation, are travelling towards God. They will be more or less near to God on their pilgrimage, depending on their degree of sincerity, of charity and of intellectual openness to the light of God. Every action intended to help a man to become better, to come nearer to God, is already part of the apostolate. It would be wrong to suppose that the apostolate only begins when we openly proclaim Jesus Christ. It should of course be directed towards proclaim-

H

ing him and disposing others to hear the proclamation. But the Kingdom of God overflows the visible frontiers of the Church. For describing the direct proclamation of Jesus Christ, the Council uses another word : evangelization, which means proclamation, particularly by the spoken word, of the message of salvation in Jesus Christ.

All apostolate is not evangelization, but all evangelization is apostolate. The apostolate is a duty incumbent on the entire Church, and hence on all members of the Body of Christ. Hence the ways in which it can be carried out are extremely diverse. There is an apostolic mission appropriate to the hierarchy, that is to say, the apostolate of the bishops, and the apostolate of priests in so far as they are the helpers of the bishops. Then there is the apostolate of members of religious orders, the apostolate of the laity, and among the laity the apostolate of individual Christians. All are sent by Christ by virtue of the mission which he has entrusted to his Church. But the responsibilities and the tasks are all different, the total mission of the Church reflecting the constituent parts of the Body of Christ, whence proceed its unity and vitality. The Church, having been instituted by Christ as a society, must use the means appropriate to any human society for ensuring her growth and the fulfilment of her mission. The Church has to have her institutions, her dioceses, her training centres, her parishes and so forth : all these are subject to human imperfection, but the need for having institutions as such cannot be held against the Church. The failure of these institutions to adapt themselves to the times is, however, quite a different thing.

There is no need here to describe the various apostolic institutions of the Church; suffice it here merely to mention one question frequently giving rise to sharp controversy : I mean, the education of children. Here we are on territory midway, you might say, between the responsibility of temporal society and the mission incumbent on the Church. Whereas the state, even when not totalitarian,

claims the education of the young as one of its own pre-
rogatives, the Church also insists on her right to educate
her Christian children. The Church's attitude on this is
often misconstrued today, often arousing sharp criticism
from Christians themselves.

Yet, to understand the Church's attitude, we have to
realize what a child is, remembering how seriously Christ
spoke of people who outrage the conscience of one of those
little ones who believe in him. The Church shares the same
fierce reactions as Christ himself, to anything threatening
the souls of children and their faith in God.

In the matter of the education of the young, responsibility
lies primarily with the parents, and remains with them,
whatever sort of education they allow their children to
have. Freedom of teaching, and freedom to teach the
Christian religion, are treated differently in different
countries, and this is as it should be. But parents themselves are the ones who remain responsible for the Christian up-bringing and Christian education of their children,
sharing this responsibility with the Church and in the
Church. People today do not always realize how strong the
influence of school attitudes can be on the minds of the
young.

I wanted to mention this particular problem, since
many of you feel concern about it and also because it can
often give rise to heated discussions not only among Christians but also at municipal, regional and national level as a
political issue. So do not jump too hastily to conclusions
about the way the Church acts over this; for the Church
can never forget the eternal dimension of her mission and
she knows from experience how the environment in which
a child grows up marks the man for life. The Church is the
mother of the divine life of her members; her reactions are
those of a mother.

I remember how sad I felt in Cuba when we were on a
tour of inspection with the head of a state farm. With us
we had a party militant who was going round the schools

giving the children lessons in atheism. An agricultural engineer who was also with us and was a Christian, took advantage of a moment when we were alone to say how horrified he was and that he considered this violation of the youthful conscience nothing short of criminal.

What about the apostolate in the modern world? People talk of a crisis in the apostolate. And this is perhaps more obviously seen in new countries that used to be missionary areas. But the crisis exists in our western, so-called Christian, countries too.

In countries that have only recently been evangelized and where the Church has only just been set up, we find a total rejection of the old-style missionary approach, and a halt to evangelism, even in some cases a sort of retreat. It is a period of transition : the first thing is for the Church to become fully the Church of the country in question. Once this has been achieved, the Church will resume her forward march. All the while the Church is not firmly rooted in a country, she cannot fully discharge her mission of evangelizing it.

In our own countries, the situation is different. We talk about the Church's failure to adapt; and the crisis in the apostolate makes itself felt primarily in a crisis of the priesthood. Many priests are no longer quite sure of the purpose for which they were ordained. Most of these were trained to minister in fully Christian conditions. Neither the organization of the Church, nor the training of future priests, was adapted to the new requirements of an evangelism, the scope of which has still to be determined.

So you can imagine the confusion and suffering that many priests are now experiencing. Laymen should try to sympathize with their priests. At the moment, the laity seems to have a more balanced view of things than the clergy does; yet the Church is in great need of priests. You might even say that it is up to the laity to retrain their priests, by showing them what they expect of them. In the interim, the crisis will inevitably be accompanied by a slowing down or even a halt in priestly vocations.

Priests now being in doubt about the practical nature of their mission, have an added difficulty in being uncertain about their status in society. No one can live without belonging to some community or other. The modern world insists, more than ever, that a man should have a station in life : and this is normally afforded by the sort of work he does. A professor has his standing in relation to his university, to his colleagues and to his pupils. Similarly, a workman or an engineer has his standing in society as determined by the job he does. The sort of work a man does usually bestows an environment as well. One of the miseries of the proletariat – among many others – is having no status vis-à-vis the society that exploits it. And what about the priest? In a Christian environment and in a Christian community, he has his position as priest. But in other circumstances, his position becomes a hard one. It can become painful, and too onerous to bear. A Christian community supports the priest because his priestly activities are necessary to that community; and the community benefits from them, recognizes their importance and wants the priest to provide them. But in a secularized, atheistical society, what is the priest to do? As priest, he might as well not exist; he has no role to play. Rather than be condemned to live in almost intolerable loneliness and frustration, he feels impelled to seek some human community to which he feels he can belong. This will probably be the company of his brother-priests, of the diocesan clergy, of the religious congregation of which he is a member. Well and good. But even while falling back on clerical society, he worries about having cut himself off from the people to whom he has been sent by virtue of his priesthood. And if contrariwise he wants to find a place in ordinary society, he may be tempted to do this by getting married and taking a job. We can only emphasize that the priest must be carried, understood, loved and supported by the Christian community.

The Church cannot live without priests. But we must quickly discover what new forms evangelism must take. The priest who feels it a vital need that he should have a working-context within the framework of society, will see this working-context as the obligatory point of departure for evangelizing the environment. There are dangers here. One is that the spiritual mission of the priesthood can evaporate in favour of purely temporal activities. The other is that it can become no more than a passive presence, heroic very possibly, a waiting for the hour of God.

In some countries, of course, where the Church finds it hard to win a footing, this sort of action on the apostle's part is justifiable. But the risk is always there of forgetting the true mission of the Church – which is to proclaim the message of Jesus Christ, to evangelize the world; and of forgetting that this mission is binding on us all, each in his own degree.

More than ever today, our living witness is what is needed for evangelism.

The evangelization of the world will never be achieved without the living witness of all Christians, without a witness truly expressing the basic teachings of the Gospel. (Equally, be it said, the way we conceive our duties and put them into practice can be counter-productive.) The apostolic obligation to bear witness affects all followers of Christ, all members of the Church, from the Pope to the layman. The outward appearance of the Church, the life-style of her hierarchy, her institutions, all these are secondary in themselves, but not for the man in search of God. Without faith, what has he to go on, if not the outward appearance of the mystery, at once living yet hidden in the Church of Jesus? The majority of people can only glimpse the mystery of the Church through its visible embodiment. The purity of the sign, the value of the witness, should preoccupy the minds of everyone who cares about the apostolate. Evangelization today depends on the witness of lives like ours.

The young Israelis were impressed by the way some Brothers lived while sharing the life and work of a kibbutz in Israel : work, chastity in celibacy, brotherly love, poverty and times devoted to prayer. "Tell us why you live like this?" they asked one of the Brothers. Lectures and sermons were not what they wanted : what they wanted was a concrete explanation of why the Brothers lived like that. And when a Brother advised them, if they were really interested, to get in touch with the religious in Tel Aviv, they said : "Doctrines and ideas are not what interest us, we want to understand your life itself." So it is important that the specifically Christian qualities should be lived courageously and unambiguously. Prayer, chastity, and a special quality of friendship are specifically Christian characteristics. The chastity of a religious or of a priest often has far wider effects that we might imagine, especially when lived with deep conviction. We must believe in what we are doing, we must believe in our Christian or our religious life. Our life must be led near people, open to their inspection, a simple, transparent life. We must be seen to live as we are.

Often enough our witness to the faith and to Christian life may pass unnoticed. In some environments there is a real indifference to any values other than materialistic ones. Many men think of nothing but money, comfort and pleasure. People can indeed be blind and deaf to the values of the Kingdom of God. Christ was aware of this : he often ended his parables and sermons with the words : *"If anyone has ears to hear, let him listen!"* (Matt. 11. 15). How mysterious life is : some men can hear the message, and others cannot !

Another essential feature of the apostolate is "poverty of means". A Church rich in institutions and in means of action or of teaching, no longer impresses the world at large. You might even say that these efficient methods act as a screen between her message and the intended recipients.

The question of what means should be used in the apostolate is not as simple as it may appear. And first of all, what
do we mean when we talk about poor means? By this,
are we to understand that the methods do not cost much,
that they are financially cheap? No, not at all. I mean
rather methods that by their nature, by their transparency,
do not form a screen obstructing the spiritual and evangelical message that they should be passing on to other
people. Rich means are high-powered means that tend to
become an object in themselves, to the detriment of the
message. Attention is drawn rather to the method than to the
message being delivered. In the ordinary course of events,
evangelization is best done by the witness of people who
have committed themselves for life to God. Some methods
tend to eliminate personal witness altogether.

The methods to be adopted for the apostolate are related
to the problem raised by some apostolic institutions of the
Church, the efficacy of which is on the wane in some
countries, if not actually at a stand-still. I remember in
Japan how some western missionaries reacted to the advice
given them by the Japanese bishop of the diocese. The
missionaries had set up house in the middle of a vast
industrial conurbation composed of little low wooden
houses typical of the country. The missionaries belonged to
a recently founded congregation, and were well-meaning,
frank, simple and full of goodwill; they did everything they
could to adapt themselves to their environment. They
lived in a Japanese-style house and had made a serious
study of the language. One day they told the bishop that
it was time for them to build a church. They had planned a
very simple building such as you can see any day in the
outskirts of a European city : a modest building in reinforced concrete with, underneath it, a parish hall. The
bishop told them that the building was too big and that
Japanese people would not like a chapel which they had to
reach by going up steps. "Instead of one church," said the
bishop, "why not make several small oratories to fit into the

general architecture of the district, with roofs that do not come above the roof-level of the neighbouring houses? This would be more in keeping with the spirit of the beatitudes." The missionaries were amazed, and decided that this plan would be much more complicated and perhaps more expensive than their ferro-concrete building; and built their church! There you have an example of what poverty of means might be: the little oratories would have been the poor method, even though more expensive.

Moreover, in the same district of the town the Baptists had their church inside a house no bigger than any of the others, with just a little wooden cross on the roof. The Protestant Korean chapel was also very humble and inconspicuous.

Another thing that might be said about evangelization in the modern world is that it has to reach people through a society. You have to have a natural community as a base for evangelization. I think this is essential. And you will find this to be so, or soon to be so, in most parishes now too vast to constitute a community of manageable size. This is my conclusion, based on numerous experiments made by the Little Brothers of the Gospel, as well as among the working-classes of Europe and Latin America, and also among primitive peoples, as for example Indian tribes in the basin of the Orinoco, and Africans too. Outside the context of a natural community, it is virtually impossible to evangelize. The Church is a society. The liturgy is prayer in common, or more accurately the prayer of a community united by the bonds of charity. But it would be wrong to think that the liturgy alone can bring this community into existence. The latter has to have its natural basis and be in existence before the liturgical assembly can be held. After that, liturgical prayer becomes the community's soul, its means of expression, and enlivens it with the spirit of Christ. No man can live in total isolation. And for this reason the Church cannot turn her back on society;

human development and evangelization are linked together, the Christian community being primarily a natural
community, though penetrated and quickened by faith in
Christ and by brotherly love. The formation of brotherly
groups, basic communities, cells of the Church, is one of the
manifestations of an authentic apostolate, and essential, in
my view, to the future of Christianity. These communities
should not be regarded as a return to a generalized
Christian society, for the world today is irrevocably plural-
istic. Nor does the idea of brotherly communities mean
that Christians are going to shut themselves up inside them
as though in ghettoes. Quite the reverse! They will have to
be out and about everywhere, in every sector of human
activity : but they cannot go on bearing fruitful witness
without belonging to a brotherly community, to a church
on a human scale.

When countries drop back from a level of practice which
entitles them to be called Christian, to a general weakening
of all that is essentially consistent with the Christian spirit,
it is no good our saying that they are still Christian
countries : the time has come to evangelize them all over
again. This sort of re-evangelization has its own quite new
set of problems. Take for instance the case of a parish in
Rio de Janeiro, situated in a gigantic shanty-town. The
parish priest is an Italian, heroic, poor, a holy priest devoted
to his people. But he still practises the old-style evangelism.
For his 15,000 parishioners he has built a big reinforced
concrete church by pinching, scraping and voluntary
labour. In this building he can accommodate everyone for
his church services. His people, who are great lovers of
ceremonies, believe in something, but not in real Christianity. You only have to walk through the lanes of the district
to realize exactly what it is that these poor people are
waiting for. For in their confused way, they are waiting to
hear the message of Christ, and there is no one to proclaim
it to them. You do not rechristianize people from the
pulpit, when you have a congregation of several thousand

people. You can preach a sermon, you can make them pray, but you cannot reconvert a people to Christianity, you cannot teach them how to live by the Gospel. It cannot be done. And so we may well wonder what ought to be done instead. In that particular district, what were needed were a hundred deacons, or priests or catechists, or even laymen, to teach the people how to find what they were looking for, by talking to individual men, women and children. In this mass of people, you would have to found small communities, aware of their own dignity and of their responsibilities, who would demonstrate that the message of Jesus, faith in him, prayer and brotherly love, when put into practice, are the true inspiration of human progress. Christian life can only flourish when it assumes responsibility for itself and for others in a brotherly community.

I could give you many similar examples. Latin America, the scene of many of them, will play a great role in the future of the Church. The people there are poor, and by taking the initiative in their own development are likely to help us discover how to set about a true evangelization : always provided of course that they have enough faith and commonsense not to let themselves be led astray by materialistic ideologies – all too often the only ones offering them the means of political and social improvement.

For some years now there has been a community of Little Sisters of the Gospel on a big island in Venezuela. The standard of living in the fishing villages there is as low as I have ever seen. In fact I have never come across such physical, moral and social misery linked to such lack of opportunity for properly remunerative work. These people need to be helped up the slope, "to stand on their own feet" to use an expression of Don Helder Camara. But they have to be helped to do it themselves, not have it done for them. And evangelization and catechesis should be part of and ancillary to, this rehabilitation. The bishop invited me to send priests for these people. I answered that priests were not immediately necessary, since the people themselves were not yet ready to receive the sacraments, for these still meant nothing to them. What they did need was a decent, responsible life; they needed to have work and, contingent on that, to have a proper family life and a sense of morality. And their own efforts needed to be supported by people who would proclaim the message of Jesus to them. They needed catechists living with them, living among them. And indeed there were young men and young women of the place who would have been willing to devote themselves to the task. But they would have needed a little training and instruction in a catechetical centre. Alas, the diocese had not as yet foreseen the need for any training centre; there wasn't one. No one had so much as realized the need for one.

These are the sort of problems presented to the contemporary evangelist : their solution lies through the means of basic communities, truly Christian and truly integrated into society. We have not yet got evangelists trained for the job, or far too few of them. But although the source of vocations to the priesthood may have dried up for the time being, I am convinced that the Church will indeed be able to find alternative means. The Church has gone through periods just as difficult in the past. But what is new now, is the urgent need for all Christians to be aware of the problem. The Church can do nothing without the laity. Now we have deacons and catechists : great efforts have been made and are being made, for instance, in the sphere of the adult catechumenate. We have already underlined the importance of temporal commitment; we must not overlook the equally urgent importance of commitment to the service of the Church, an obligation binding on each of us.

Every Christian, everyone who believes in Jesus Christ as Saviour, has a duty to bear witness to his faith and to confess it openly when this is demanded of him. We must be careful not to hide from the people among whom we live that one thing that they, whether consciously or unconsciously, expect from us. We cannot limit ourselves to a concern for their standard of living, and their economic and even moral needs. We must be brothers to them too, in all that concerns their deeper spritual needs and their progress towards God.

Evangelization begins as soon as a man starts trying to live his life by the Gospel, even though he may not yet have encountered Christ in faith. This is how evangelization has to begin. This is what John the Baptist did, and Jesus himself, when he began by teaching the claims of the Kingdom of God to the crowd before asking them (as he had already asked his Apostles) to believe in him as Son of God.

We can, and we must, help people to live according to the Gospel, even before we can talk to them about the Lord. There are such qualities as peace, brotherly love and courage in times of ordeal, which can transform the heart and predispose it to faith. It is not enough merely to teach the content of the faith : we must teach them to have evangelical reflexes. And that can only be done in the environment of a small, friendly group or of a brotherly community. This indeed is how the primitive Church came into existence. The first Christians gathered in one house, round one family : then the message of the Gospel was handed on from group to group. And these groups in turn grew into local Churches. And thus the Church was born : and thus, I believe, in our own very different world, the Church will be born again.

Just as temporal commitment is obligatory to every man aware of his human responsibilities, so apostolic commitment is obligatory to every Christian aware of his responsibilities as a member of the Body of Christ. Every Christian should decide what his temporal or apostolic duties are to be in the light of his own talents, vocation and position in the city or in the Church. And the young, most especially, should be brought up to discharge their political, social and Christian responsibilities. You cannot train a Christian without training a man – in the fullest sense of the word. All catechesis should have this in mind. An immense task awaits Christians and all men of goodwill in the world of tomorrow.

*   *   *   *   *

.In the Church there are two observable tendencies in the way Christians live their spiritual life. On the one hand, there is the tendecy to uniformity, to a sort of standardization. On the other there is a tendency to a more personal approach.

The tendency towards standardization of spiritual training lays emphasis on Church and liturgical life as the unique source and expression of Christian living. It attaches little importance to, and sometimes even questions the acceptability of, having many different religious orders, spiritual families and the various spiritualities deriving from them. It would seem preferable to have what is called "a Christian spirituality"; and as a sign of progress, to return to the simplicity of a single spirituality such as animated the Christian community in primitive times. Liturgical renewal, as principal source of life and prayer, clearly emphasizes the basic unity of Christian spirituality. But without at all disputing the fundamental need for this unity, differing forms of spirituality have an important future too.

Unity is not the same as uniformity; and if unity is a living thing, it naturally engenders variety. Spiritual life is profoundly affected by culture and personality. No two men on earth live the Gospel in the same way, and the more deeply the Gospel permeates our life and our being, the more personal a form it assumes.

We each have needs that are not the same as our neighbour's. Our vocation, not only our human vocation but our spiritual vocation, inclines us to some particular aspect of a spirituality as vast and full of unexplored riches as the very mystery of Christ from whom it proceeds. Within the same culture, the kind of work you do and the kind of commitments you make contribute to making your spiritual life different from anyone else's. An attempt to impose a uniform spirituality would either be doomed to failure or would have the effect of sterilizing all efforts towards a deep personal relationship with God. Recently a priest from a diocese in Andalusia confided in me that for many years he had been struggling against a temptation to join an association of priests, for fear of cutting himself off from the other priests of the diocese; but that he could not go on resisting any more, since he felt such an intense need for the spirituality and the support of the association in question. I encouraged him not to go on struggling, since it was not a temptation at all but a call from the Holy Spirit. The unity of the clergy is the fruit of the charity and spiritual good-health of its members, not of some notion of uniformity. All free life is multiform and unpredictable. You might as well try to standardize feelings, art and poetry: you would not need much standardization to kill the deeper life of man; for this can only flourish in freedom of spirit and freedom of heart.

Moreover, the greater the tendency of civilization and culture to standardize attitudes of mind, behaviour and environments, the greater the reaction against this will be, being the reflex actions of human personality striving to be true to itself.

Regionalism, language revivals and renewed interest in folklore all bear witness to this same tendency in modern life: man needs an environment of his own scale in which he can be fully himself. And the history of the various forms of spirituality in the Church shows how diversity contributes to fulness of life.

A plurality of spiritual families is not only justifiable but actually necessary to the fulfilling and deepening of Christian life. And the Lord himself was in fact the one who instituted these life-giving currents in the Church and raised up the saints to give them vigour. The role of the Church is to authenticate these currents by purifying them of error, of falsehood and of deviation introduced by human limitation.